Longman State Politics Series

California

Eighth Edition

Pamela Fiber-Ostrow
California State University, Fullerton

Longman

Boston   Columbus   Indianapolis   New York   San Francisco   Upper Saddle River

Amsterdam   Cape Town   Dubai   London   Madrid   Milan   Munich   Paris   Montreal   Toronto

Delhi   Mexico City   São Paulo   Sydney   Hong Kong   Seoul   Singapore   Taipei   Tokyo

California (Longman State Politics Series), Eighth Edition

14 EBM 18 17 16 15

Longman
is an imprint of

www.pearsonhighered.com

ISBN 10: 0-205-06669-0
ISBN 13: 978-0-205-06669-8

Table of Contents

CHAPTER 1: *INTRODUCTION TO CALIFORNIA POLITICS*

INTRODUCTION

"It's 90 degrees in November, the full glory and perennial curse of Southern California on fierce display. Devil winds, hill-hopping infernos, smoked mansions, torched trailers, barren freeways, and brilliant sunsets lingering in low-hanging canopies of burnt dreams. Are we all crazy? Don't live here, says the wind, the trembling earth, the parched land whose natural inclination is to explode in flame every year about now. But we do. Don't build near the kindling, say the voices of common sense. But we do, for all the wrong reasons and all the known glories. Our winter snowfall is flakes of ash and flame retardant falling on bougainvillea, so it could be worse. The Earth shakes. The fires rage. The population expands. And the sunsets are brilliant, especially this time of year."
> -Steve Lopez, columnist for the *Los Angeles Times* November 17, 2008

"Everyone is welcome. As you know, I'm an immigrant. I came over here as an immigrant. What gave me the opportunities, what made me be able to be here today, is the open arms of Americans. I have been received. I have been adopted to America. I have gotten all the opportunities because of America. I have seen first hand, coming over here, with empty pockets, but full of dreams, full of desire, full of will, to succeed. But with the opportunities that I had available, I could make it. And that's what I want everyone to be able to do. This is why we have to get back and bring California back where it once was."
> – Arnold Schwarzenegger, upon announcing his intention to run for governor of California in 2003

The state of California has been the pace-setter for political, cultural, and technological development in the nation, where dreams begin and are realized. California has a rich political history, a remarkably diverse population, and an exciting future. The Golden State is literally and symbolically a global phenomenon. It is both the most populous state and the most diverse; its people match its geology. In terms of economics, it is an international force in trade and commerce, higher education, scientific research, entertainment, and technology. However, the same features that drive its success also present a host of challenges; the abundance of opportunities are attended with challenges in energy production, environmental protection, elementary and secondary education, social services, general health, and the well-being of the population.

CALIFORNIA'S POLITICAL CULTURE

Political culture is the set of ideas and values Americans share about who should govern, for what ends, and by what means. California's political culture is characterized by the settlement patterns that occurred during nineteenth- and twentieth-century migration. Political scientist Daniel Elazar recognized that while the United States shares a general political culture, three distinct subcultures can be identified. These cultures were established at the earliest founding of the nation and were distributed geographically with

1

the migration of the founders and their progeny. The shared culture is characterized by the tension between viewing the political arena as a marketplace as opposed to a commonwealth. The typology of culture Elazar introduces reflects the sociocultural differences of immigrants settling in the states. The three subcultures identified are moralistic, individualistic, and traditionalistic.[1] Each subculture has a unique value system that shapes the ways in which individuals view political competition, policy goals, and the roles of the citizen within the polity.

According to the theories, the individualist sees the political system as a marketplace established for utilitarian purposes. As such, the role of government should be limited, and personal freedom is revered as the primary attribute of society. The role of the individual in politics is characterized by what the player will gain from participation. The quest for self-interest makes politics a dirty business. For this reason, corruption in government and politics is generally expected.

Much in contrast to the individualist, the moralistic culture sees the political arena as a commonwealth. For the moralist, politics is the search for the "good society." Individual participation is not only encouraged, but expected, as it is the civic duty of every citizen in the advancement of society. Contrary to the individualist, the government is a positive instrument with the responsibility to promote the general welfare, rejecting the notion that politics is the forum for self-interest. For this reason, there is no room for corruption. The government takes an active role, allowing for intervention into the economic and social life of the community, in pursuit of the common good.

Finally, the traditionalist culture, very distinct from the other two, is characterized by an ambivalent attitude toward the marketplace, and it embodies a paternalistic and elitist conception of the commonwealth. The traditionalist accepts hierarchical society as part of the "ordered nature of things." For the traditionalist, the role of government is to maintain the status quo, with political power confined to a small group of elites in society. Individuals are not encouraged, nor are they expected to participate in government; thus politics is characterized by nepotism in a single-party system.

Elazar's geographical mappings feature California as a mixture of individualistic and moralistic cultures, which often exist in tension. These tensions are evident in policy debates in California's legislature and in popular initiatives proposed and enacted by the people. California's 1994 smoking ban illustrates these tensions. The ensuing debate pitted a community's desire for a healthy environment against individual smokers who felt their rights were under assault, and from bar owners who wanted to protect their profits by catering to smokers.

California's Individualistic Culture

Various regions within California display these differing cultures. The southern part of the state was settled by white Protestants from the Midwest, Great Plains, and South, who immigrated to southern California from the late nineteenth century to the middle of the

---

[1] Daniel Elazar, 1966. *American Federalism: A View From the States*. New York: Thomas Y. Crowell Company.

twentieth century, making it the most conservative part of the state. Following this influx, anticommunist conservatives and the John Birch Society began settling in southern California during the 1950s and 1960s, and middle- and upper-class whites who found work in the defense and manufacturing industries after World War II purchased homes in suburban Orange County. Several factors contributed to California's individualistic leanings during the mid-twentieth century, including a large white population, migration of World War II veterans, affordable home ownership, economic growth and prosperity, and Protestantism.[2] The conservatism of southern California is mitigated by the increase in minorities in the region. African Americans who were affected by the Great Depression came to southern California seeking jobs following World War II and settled into the urban centers. Additionally, Latino and Asian immigrants joined an existing community of Latinos in urban Los Angeles and its surroundings further moderating the conservatism of the area.

The Central Valley has economic and settlement roots in agriculture and was predominantly a conservative Democratic area; however this has changed with migration of whites from the coastal regions of California and increases in Republican registration are more common. The region is characterized by a migration of people from Oklahoma and Arkansas during the Dust Bowl and Great Depression. Its political culture reflects the dominance of agribusiness and a large white population.[3]

California's Moralistic Culture

Northern California and the Bay Area are characterized by Elazar's moralistic culture. The Gold Rush invited immigrants from across the United States and beyond as Italian, Irish, German, and Chinese immigrants sought to enjoy the boom. Explanations for its liberalism and communal perspective include explosive growth during the nineteenth century, its role as a major seaport and international outlook, and settlement by New Englanders. Just as southern California's conservatism has been moderated by the heterogeneity of its inhabitants, so too is northern California's liberalism mitigated by high-tech industry in the Silicon Valley and suburbs.

California's Ideological Diversity

Elazar's typology aside, California's voting habits reflect the various ideological and religious influences of the settlement patterns discussed above. The map below, which shows support for Proposition 8 that appeared on the November 4, 2008 ballot (more detail in Chapter 4), is illustrative. The measure changed the California Constitution to eliminate the right of same-sex couples to marry in California by providing that only marriage between a man and a woman is valid or recognized in California.

---

[2] John Heppen, 2001. "The Changing Political Landscape of California 1968 to 2000." *Yearbook of The Association of Pacific Coast Geographers*. Volume 63, 29.
[3] John Heppen, 2001. "The Changing Political Landscape of California 1968 to 2000." *Yearbook of The Association of Pacific Coast Geographers*. Volume 63, 31.

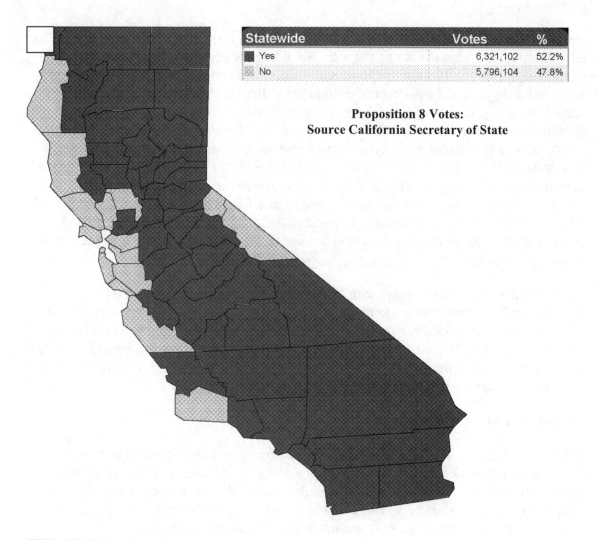

Statewide	Votes	%
Yes	6,321,102	52.2%
No	5,796,104	47.8%

Proposition 8 Votes:
Source California Secretary of State

THE PEOPLE OF CALIFORNIA

Population

While it is only the third-largest state in terms of land area, California supports the largest population in the nation. This affords California the largest delegation to the House of Representatives (53), and the largest allocation of votes in the Electoral College (55). As of September 2010, California's population exceeded 38.64 million people, according to the state Department of Finance's estimates, just over a 1 percent increase from the previous year.[4] Californians represent nearly one in eight Americans, comprising 12.5 percent of the U.S. population. The figure reflects an increase of 393,000 new residents between 2008 and 2009; this figure continued the pattern of slower growth rates each year since the year 2000, when California saw an increase of 2 percent. The highest population growth rates have occurred mainly in the Central Valley and foothill counties and in Riverside and San Bernardino Counties in southern California.

---

[4] State of California, Department of Finance, *Current Population Survey: California Two-year Average Series: March 2000-2009 Data*. Sacramento, California. September 2010

California's Cities. California currently boasts 21 cities with populations exceeding 200,000, with Oxnard topping 200,000 and the city of Fresno exceeding 500,000 in 2009. Los Angeles is home to over 4.095 million residents, and San Diego is the second largest city with 1.38 million residents, according to California's Department of Finance.[5] The housing market has affected population growth as the economy struggles to grow and this is reflected in California's five fastest growing cities: The Department of Finance ranked The City of Colfax in Placer County the fastest growing city in California, (+5.7 percent) with Beaumont in Riverside County (+5.5 percent), Sand City in Monterey County (+5.4 percent), Coachella in Riverside County (+3.8 percent), and Oakley in Contra Costa County (+3.3 percent) following closely behind. As the DOF explains, "These cities added a proportionally large number of new residents from recent housing increases or from occupancy resulting from previously reported housing units."[6]

California's Counties. Of California's ten most populated counties, nine have over 1 million residents and these ten counties include Los Angeles, Orange, San Diego, San Bernardino, Riverside, Santa Clara, Alameda, Sacramento, Contra Costa, and Fresno, at nearly 900,000 residents. The counties of Orange and San Diego each exceed 3 million, and 10,341,410 call Los Angeles County home, which is the most populous county in the nation, representing over 28 percent of the state's population. The county of Alpine is the smallest, with 1,208.[7]

Ethnic Groups

People from all parts of the world have come to California, drawn by its opportunities for economic success. California's governor, Arnold Schwarzenegger, an immigrant himself, made many references to his own California dream during his bid for governor. The original Native Americans have become a very small percentage of the population, one of many ethnic minorities in California. While tribal members represent less than 1 percent of the population, their 200,000 plus members are the largest such group in any state. Non-Latino whites are still the largest demographic group in the state, although the estimates from Department of Finance revealed that they constitute 40.83 percent of the population, far from an absolute majority of the residents of the Golden State. The fastest growing ethnic groups in California include Hispanic (+4.7 percent), Asian (+1.36 percent), Pacific Islander (+0.05 percent), and Multirace (+1.0 percent).[8]

One out of every four Californians was born outside the United States, a fact reflected by the population's racial, ethnic, linguistic, and cultural richness.[9] The state also sustains major populations of Iranian, Armenian, Asian Indian, Vietnamese, and other populations, the vast majority of them first-generation immigrants.

---

[5] California Department of Finance "Report: California Added 393,000 in 2009; Population Tops 38.6 Million" April 10, 2010

[6] Ibid page 1

[7] State of California, Department of Finance, *California County Race / Ethnic Population Estimates and Components of Change by Year, July 1, 2000–2008.* Sacramento, California, June 2010.

[8] State of California, Department of Finance, *California County Race / Ethnic Population Estimates and Components of Change by Year, July 1, 2000–2008.* Sacramento, California, June 2010.

[9] Kevin Starr, "California: the Dream and the Challenge in the Twenty-first Century." History of California, http://www.ca.gov.

Immigrants. California's census information is updated every ten years along with the federal census. The most current information is from 2002 and indicates that 49 percent of the state's 2002 immigrants were born in Latin America and the Caribbean, primarily Mexico, and almost 40 percent were born in Asia, including the Philippines, People's Republic of China, India, Vietnam, Iran, Korea, and Taiwan.[10] Immigrant population growth averaged about 6.3 per 1,000 annually accounting for a 4.1 percent increase in California.

Latinos. Residents of Latino heritage (3.1 million) represent about one-third of the population of California in 2009. This increase is largely due to new births in California (70 percent). While Los Angeles has one of the largest Mexican populations,[11] the Hispanic population grew in every county. According to California's Department of Finance, Los Angeles, Orange, and San Bernardino Counties had the largest increases, while Imperial County in the far southern part of the state continued to have the highest percentage, reaching 72 percent by the year 2000. Central California's Latinos have influence in this region due to farm labor union activism and a growing urban population with increased political clout. The majority of Hispanics trace their heritage to Mexico. Mexican Americans have traditionally come for economic reasons. From 1951 to 1964, the governments of the United States and Mexico had a formal agreement to permit Mexican workers, or "braceros," to enter the U.S. legally to work in the fields of California farms. This program was abandoned, however, under pressure from organized labor. Since then, the flow of immigrants seeking a better life has not halted; the United States has simply made it illegal.

The 1980s ushered in a new wave of immigrants in California from Central America. In countries such as El Salvador, Nicaragua, and Guatemala, political unrest, civil war, and economic devastation forced large numbers to seek safety and asylum elsewhere. Many of these immigrants came as political refugees; others followed unlawful paths across the border.

The flood of Spanish-speaking immigrants created tension among Californians. Through the initiative process, California voters have passed numerous laws aimed at these groups. Proposition 38 in 1984 required all voting materials to be printed in English only, but the law was invalidated because it conflicted with federal law. Also meaningless was Proposition 63 in 1986, which declared English the official language of California. In 1994, the people of California passed Proposition 187, which forbade children living in California illegally to enroll in public schools and denied welfare to illegal residents. Ultimately, the federal government adopted the welfare provisions, and federal courts declared the education provisions unconstitutional.

Asians. While Caucasians and Latinos represent the largest ethnic groups in California, residents of Asian origin are the fastest-growing population. Chinese immigrants arrived in California during the Gold Rush, while many more were brought to the state in the

---

[10] State of California, Department of Finance, *Legal Immigration to California in 2002*. Sacramento, California, October 2003.

[11] Kevin Starr, "California: the Dream and the Challenge in the Twenty-first Century." History of California, http://www.ca.gov.

1860s to work on the railroad. Japanese and Filipino immigrants arrived later in the early part of the twentieth century. Koreans, Taiwanese, Thais, and Pacific Islanders have all followed. One of the more notable influxes was that of the Vietnamese, who came following the fall of Saigon. Camp Pendleton was the west coast port of entry for refugees fleeing the communist government, and many stayed to become residents and citizens of California. Over a million Chinese Americans and over a million Filipino Americans reside in California. Asians grew from 11 percent to 12.4 percent of the state's total, increasing by about 966,000.[12]

The United States has not always been friendly to immigrants from the Far East. In 1881, Congress passed the Chinese Exclusion Act, which temporarily halted immigration from China. In 1924, Congress passed the National Immigration Act, which effectively halted Japanese immigration. In California, laws passed in the Progressive Era banned land ownership by aliens, and the incarceration of Japanese residents during World War II is a painful part of our history. Nevertheless, Asian Americans have become a vital and important part of the California cultural and economic landscape.

Pacific Islanders. Pacific Islanders comprise the smallest percentage of the census tracking in California They accounted for just a 0.37 percent share of the state population in 2008, adding about 31,000 people.

African Americans. During World War II, large numbers of Southern blacks left their homes to seek urban jobs created by the booming war economy. Many came to California and settled in urban areas in southern California, where the black population grew steadily from the 1940s to the 1960s. The percentage of Blacks in the state has dropped to 5.8 percent from 6.5 percent in 2000.

Of the minority groups in California, African Americans achieved political success earlier than other groups. At the state level, the longest-serving speaker of the assembly was Willie Brown, a black attorney from San Francisco. In Congress, in the legislature, and on city councils, black officials have been prominent for years. Tom Bradley, Los Angeles' first African American mayor and the first black mayor of a major city who served an unprecedented five terms, was elected during the social and political turmoil of the early 1970s. Indeed, today there are emerging political problems, as cities such as Inglewood and Compton continue to be governed by blacks, while their populations become increasingly Latino.

Multirace. California's census has also followed the increase in residents reporting a mixed race background. People of mixed race account for about 2.8 percent of California's population, growing to about 1.1 million people from under 650,000 in 2000.

In much of the rest of the country, the topic of race relations refers primarily to blacks and whites. California is much more diverse. The state was Spanish, then Mexican, then American, and now includes a rich mix of Latino, Caucasian, Asian, black, and Native

---

[12] State of California, Department of Finance, *California County Race / Ethnic Population Estimates and Components of Change by Year, July 1, 2000–2008.* Sacramento, California, June 2010.

American peoples. With this incredible diversity, the state has entered the twenty-first century.

THE GEOGRAPHY

California has 58 counties, covering a wide array of topography and geology. The north-south boundary of California commonly divides California along the Tehachapi Mountains, separating the counties of San Luis Obispo, Kern, and San Bernardino in the south, from Monterey, Kings, Tulare, and Inyo counties to the north. San Diego and Imperial Counties border with Mexico. The state stretches 825 miles from its northwest corner on the Pacific Ocean to its southeast corner at the junction of the Gila and Colorado Rivers. The winding shoreline contains 1,264 miles of beaches and harbors. Elevations run from 14,495 feet at the peak of Mount Whitney to 282 feet below sea level at Death Valley, sites barely 50 miles apart in Inyo County.

California has extremes in all directions. Mountain ranges flank California on the coasts and borders, creating peaks and valleys that provide both extremely fertile and arid soil in the valleys and inclement weather and infertile lands in the deserts. Channels of rivers provide nourishment for the valley lands. California's northern border with Oregon runs through the Klamath and Cascade Mountains and the Modoc Plateau. The Sacramento Valley runs south from the highlands, and the San Joaquin Rivers, extending 400 miles, are bounded by the Coastal Mountains on the west and the Sierra Nevadas on the east. The Sierra Nevadas, extend 400 miles south from Lawson Peak to Tejon Pass in Los Angeles County. East of the southern Sierra Nevadas are the mountains of the Great Basin, with the Sierras and Basin ranges bounded on the south by the Mojave Desert and the Salton Sea.[13]

The topography creates a variety of climates. High mountain ranges experience heavy snows, while the coast enjoys more mild and temperate weather. The various valleys offer wide variations in temperature and humidity, with arid conditions and great temperature fluctuations in the desert. The available arid land has been a boon for California's economy and contributes to California's global presence. Its economy is the largest among the states and in terms of gross domestic product (GDP), ranks California among the biggest producers in the world.

NATURAL DISASTERS

California's diverse landscape also invites a host of disasters that present policy issues for California's decision makers. Perhaps globally, California is known for its earthquakes and fires although various regions have seen floods and frosts so severe as to destroy over half the agriculture revenue expected for a season.

Records of California's earthquakes date back as early as 1769 as detailed by the U.S. Geological Survey. Many of the major quakes have fallen along the San Andreas Fault, which runs about 800 miles from northern California to southern California, with active

---

[13] Kevin Starr, "California: the Dream and the Challenge in the Twenty-first Century." History of California, http://www.ca.gov.

fault lines branching out throughout the state. Policymakers obviously can do nothing to prevent quakes, but they can make decisions regarding building safety, emergency procedures, and even insurance policy requirements for victims of major earthquakes.

California has experienced devastating fires due to a confluence of factors including rising annual temperatures resulting in drought, high winds known as Santa Ana winds, diseased trees due to the bark beetle, lightning, and even arson. The year 2007 brought some of the most devastating fires to southern California. The Insurance Information Institute estimated that insured damages cost over $500 million. Over 1,300 homes were destroyed, at least five people died, and over 1 million people were evacuated. Sixteen separate fires were blazing through Orange, San Diego and Santa Barbara Counties, fanned by winds gusting up to 60 mph. In November 2008 southern Californians experienced another set of blazes in Santa Barbara, Orange County, and Los Angeles Counties, and over 900 structures were lost. The state must reconcile how to pay for the damages, mitigate the insurance losses, and investigate and prosecute any incidences of arson and negligence; in addition, the state will have to explore ways to improve California's fire responses. Californians will have to pick up their lives through the ashes and find ways to rebuild.

California is also vulnerable to flooding across the state. The area between the Sacramento and San Joaquin river floodplains are now identified as being at risk to extensive flooding, leading to great loss of life and billions of dollars in damages.[14] The United States Department of Homeland Security tracks declared disasters – that is, those disasters that a state declares to receive assistance. Between 2005 and fall 2010 there were five declarations of "Severe Storms, Flooding, Debris Flows, and Mudslides" in California, with two in 2005 and two in 2006 covering over ten different counties.

THE ECONOMY

California's economy has received significant global exposure. On a variety of measures, California leads the nation in exports, and its share of U.S. exports regularly exceeds its share of the national economy. According to the California Department of Finance, if California were an independent nation, it would have the seventh-largest economy in the world, with a gross state product of $1.850 trillion according to a study by RAND.[15]

California's Agriculture

Agriculture is California's leading industry, and the Golden State is the biggest agricultural producer and exporter in the United States. According to California's Department of Food and Agriculture, in 2008 California's agriculture accounted for $36.2 billion in revenue.[16] This amount represented over 11 percent of the national total, and far greater than the second and third agricultural states, Iowa ($24.8 billion) and Texas ($19.2 billion). California accounted for 14 percent of national receipts for crops,

---

[14] "A California Challenge: Flooding in the Central Valley," commissioned by California's Department of Water Resources.

[15] http://ca.rand.org/stats/economics/gspnaics.html

[16] *Top California Agricultural Products by Sales 2002.*

and 7.5 percent of the U.S. revenue for livestock and livestock products. California is a major producer of 400 different crops. The state produces nearly half of U.S.- grown fruits, nuts, and vegetables. The state is a dominant producer of many specialty crops, including strawberries, kiwis, artichokes, brussels sprouts, almonds, dates, figs, nectarines, olives, pistachios, dried plums (prunes), and walnuts. California's top twenty crop and livestock commodities accounted for more than $29.6 billion in value for 2008.

According to the 2007 Census of Agriculture's ranking of market value of agricultural products sold, nine of the Nation's top ten producing counties are in California. Fresno County boasted the highest agricultural value in the nation in 2008, with $5.67 billion, followed by Tulare and Kern. Roughly 14 percent of California's agricultural production is exported[17] and over half the foreign markets are accounted for by Canada, the European Union, and Japan.

California's Nonagricultural Economy

California's nonagricultural industry has incurred several transitions, resulting from changing international conditions and natural and manmade disasters, as well as economic upturns and opportunities. Following the end of the Cold War, defense spending waned and the federal government reduced procurement and initiated many base closures; California experienced significant downsizing of its aerospace industry and reductions in Department of Defense payrolls. However, electronics manufacturing following World War II and the Cold War gave rise to the electronics and computer industries. The downsizing of the aerospace industry was met with an increase in California's role in high-technology industries in the 1990s.[18] During the latter half of the 1990s, California's economy grew faster than the nation as a whole with the dot-com boom, so called for the rise in Internet-based technology. The development of the Internet and the decrease in the cost of computer chip technology led to a boom in various high-technology fields, including computer services such as software and programming. Computer-related services proliferated to support the demands from personal computers, personal communications devices, and Internet business activities. California's Department of Finance likened the Silicon Valley of the 1990s to the nineteenth-century Gold Rush. [19] However, the productivity of Internet sales dampened, and Silicon Valley and the computer-based industry began to wane. In 2002 manufacturing employment fell, reflecting losses in the aerospace sector and declines in the commercial high-technology sector.[20]

California also draws significant revenue from tourism. Travel spending in California reached $82.5 billion in 2004, a 7.4 percent increase over the preceding year. Los Angeles County receives the most tourism in the state. Local governments generated $1.9 billion in taxes from travel spending, while the state saw $3.3 billion in revenues. For every $100 of travel spending in 2004, $32.13 was generated in earnings, $2.33 in local

---

[17] *California Agricultural Statistics Report 2003*, California Department of Food and Agriculture.
[18] California Department of Finance, *A Brief History of the California Economy.*
[19] California Department of Finance, *A Brief History of the California Economy.*
[20] *Cal Facts 2002 and Cal Facts 2004,* Legislative Analyst's Office.

taxes, and \$3.97 in state taxes.[21] California's 2004 domestic market share of tourism was 10.8 percent, and visitor volume growth, at 4.8 percent, exceeded the national average.

THE FUTURE OF CALIFORNIA POLITICS

As California faces the twenty-first century, it must meet the changing and growing demands of its citizens. Immigration and the issues attendant to public service continue to challenge California's government. Skyrocketing costs in housing provide incentives to home ownership but also make that dream impossible for all but the wealthy. Cultural and racial diversity must become a source of strength, not a justification for culture wars. Law and policy in California must balance the needs of attracting and retaining businesses while protecting its precious resources and environment.

SOMETHING TO THINK ABOUT

1. In what ways is California's political culture (individualism and moralism) reflected in politics and policy and in the people's attitudes and expectations about government?

2. What advantages does California enjoy in being the most populous state in the union?

3. What advantages does California enjoy in its wide diversity in geography?

4. What challenges does California's ethnic and cultural diversity pose in terms of politics and policy?

5. Which industries are essential to continuing California's status as an economic leader in the country and the world?

MULTIPLE-CHOICE QUESTIONS

1) Political culture refers to
   a) the ethnic make-up of the population that is reflected in popular cultural events.
   b) the culture of the political system, including who runs for office and who votes.
   c) the belief system of the founding members of the state government.
   d) the ways in which politicians interact with each other in government.
   e) the set of ideas and values Americans share about who should govern, for what ends, and by what means.

---

[21] "Tourism Continues to Boost California Economy in 2004 - New California Travel Statistics Show Upswing," California Tourism Commission.

2) Southern California's political culture is best described as
   a) individualistic and very liberal, resulting from the migration of white Protestants from the Midwest, Great Plains, and the South.
   b) individualistic and conservative, reflecting both a backlash against communism and the opportunities for jobs in the defense industry.
   c) moralistic and fairly liberal, reflecting the migration of white Protestants from the Midwest, Great Plains, and the South.
   d) individualistic and liberal, resulting from the migration of New Englanders.
   e) traditionalistic, reflecting the beliefs of conservative Democrats as a result of the dominance of agriculture.

3) Moralistic culture is best described as
   a) viewing the political arena as a commonwealth, where citizens are expected to participate for the good of every individual and society.
   b) viewing the political arena as a marketplace where cheating is immoral.
   c) viewing the political arena as a place best suited for the powerful and the rich.
   d) those areas in southern California settled by white Protestants and embodying the culture of former governor and president Ronald Reagan.
   e) emphasizing the Protestant morals and values.

4) California's demographics are best summed up as follows:
   a) The numeric majority of the population is still white, but the Latino population is increasing the fastest due to large numbers of immigrants moving to California.
   b) There is no numeric majority, but the Latino population is currently the largest ethnic group in the state.
   c) There is no numeric majority; although whites comprise the largest percentage of the population, Latinos have surpassed one-third of the population, an increase due largely to new births in the state.
   d) Whites are now outnumbered by Latinos and Asians, who are the fastest growing ethnic population in the state.
   e) Whites and African Americans comprise the two largest portions of the state's population, while Asians and Latinos are the two fastest growing populations.

5) California has been
   a) welcoming towards immigrants, as is evident in the agreements the U.S. has made with other countries to allow immigrants to work in the state.
   b) welcoming towards immigrants, expanding social service programs to include the children of immigrants and publishing official documents in multiple languages.
   c) hostile towards immigrants, requiring English tests in order to become residents of the state.
   d) welcoming towards immigrants by giving itself the nickname "the Melting Pot State."
   e) hostile to immigrants, passing initiatives restricting the use of languages other than English on official state documents and refusing social service programs.

6) In California, African Americans have served the state in a variety of ways except as
   a) a mayor of a major city.
   b) a United States representative.
   c) speaker of the state assembly.
   d) governor of the state.
   e) city council member.

7) California has _____ counties, the largest of which is _____ and the smallest of which is _____.
   a) 58; Los Angeles; Alpine
   b) 53; Los Angeles, Imperial
   c) 50; Los Angeles; Imperial
   d) 52; Los Angeles; Alameda
   e) 54; Los Angeles; Fresno

8) California's economy is highly dependent on its agriculture, which
   a) is the third biggest agricultural producer and exporter in the United States next to Texas and Iowa.
   b) is largely cattle and poultry, followed by dairy products.
   c) is the biggest agricultural producer and exporter in the United States, earning more than the two next biggest producers, Texas and Iowa, combined.
   d) represents over 25 percent of the nation's total in revenue.
   e) None of the above

9) California's population is influenced by
   a) immigration.
   b) topography.
   c) geography.
   d) agriculture.
   e) All of the above

10) California's nonagricultural economy
   a) changed dramatically after the Cold War.
   b) reflects shifts in global climate.
   c) has been very steady since World War II.
   d) is similar to the Gold Rush of the nineteenth century.
   e) is largely dependent on tourism.

INTERNET SOURCES

State of California: **http://www.ca.gov/state/portal/myca_homepage.jsp**
California Statistical Abstract: **http://www.dof.ca.gov/HTML/FS_DATA/STAT-ABS/Toc_xls.htm**
California's Legislative Analyst's Office: **http://www.lao.ca.gov/**
United States Census Bureau: **http://www.census.gov**
Department of Finance: **http://www.dof.ca.gov/html/Demograp/druhpar.htm**
Public Policy Institute of California: **http://www.ppic.org**

CHAPTER 2: *THE CALIFORNIA CONSTITUTION*

INTRODUCTION

"All political power is inherent in the people."[22]

THE FIRST TWO CONSTITUTIONS GOVERNING CALIFORNIA

Constitutional Precursors

As the United States moved west under its concept of manifest destiny, conflict with Mexico was inevitable. Mexico's independence from Spanish rule in 1822 offered unanticipated opportunities for the United States. Although Mexico's newly established Constitution of 1837 conferred considerable authority to the Governor of California, Mexico was unable to halt the advance of American interests. The Mexican-American War began in Texas in 1846, eventually leading to control over California by the United States; the symbol of American authority was embodied in raising the American flag in Monterey in 1846. The U.S. presence was comprised of a military authority, but Californians were promised constitutional rights, privileges, and law. Many Californians objected to military rule and insisted upon immediate provisions for civil government. Mexico ceded California to the United States under the Treaty of Guadalupe Hidalgo, ratified in 1848. However, following the peace treaty, California had a weak governing structure and ambiguous laws with very little formal structure of government.

During the same year, gold was discovered at Sutter's Mill on the American River. The Gold Rush beckoned to people from all over the world, who came to California seeking instant wealth. The population exploded, and the on-rushing Americans swamped the lingering Mexican and Indian influences, changing local conditions. The explosion in population outpaced the establishment of law and law enforcement. The rapid pace of settlement in California and the absence of effective laws and governance of rules led to the establishment of a civil government based upon the concepts of the common law.[23]

The United States Congress had failed to provide California with a temporary governing structure, so Californians took control. California's first constitution was drafted by 48 delegates in Monterey on September 1, 1849, a year before California was admitted into the union. The constitution was closely modeled after the constitutions of Iowa and New York, and also included influences from the constitutions of Louisiana, Wisconsin, Michigan, Texas, Mississippi, and the United States, making California a "free" state, prohibiting slavery.

The Constitution of 1849

The constitution, as framed by the Convention of 1849, established both federal and state officers. The constitution established separation of powers, and the election of a

---

[22] California Constitution, Article II, Section 1.

[23] California's Constitution from California's Historical Background—California Legislative Counsel, http://www.leginfo.ca.gov/califleg.html.

governor, a lieutenant governor, two representatives in Congress, 16 state senators, and 36 members of the assembly, comprising the first state legislature. The term of office for all of the elected officials was two years, except the assembly members, who were elected annually. The constitution included a statement that, "All political power is inherent in the people. Government is instituted for the protection, security, and benefit of the people; and they have the right to alter or reform the same, whenever the public good may require it."[24]

In terms of its admission to the union, California became the thirty-first state in the union and the sixteenth to prohibit slavery, tipping the balance of power to the free states. The bill admitting California to the union was passed by the U.S. Senate on August 13, 1850, and by the House of Representatives on September 7, 1850. On September 9, 1850, President Fillmore signed the bill granting California statehood.

The Constitution of 1879

Soon after the enactment of the Constitution of 1849, it became clear that it would be unable to meet the demands imposed upon the state by issues of taxation, big business, and the increasing power of the railroads. Delegates met and agreed upon a new constitution in 1879.

Among other changes, the new constitution provided a Declaration of Rights resembling the federal Bill of Rights. The provisions of the new constitution reaffirmed the assertion of the Constitution of 1849: "All political power is inherent in the people. Government is instituted for their protection, security, and benefit, and they have the right to alter or reform it when the public good may require."[25] In addition, the new constitution set the numbers for legislative apportionment to 80 assembly members and 40 senators, where it remains today. In addition, it amended the terms of office for the various elected officials.

The Constitution of 1879 has been significantly amended from its original document. By 1962, 583 amendments proposed by the legislature and by the people were considered, and of these, 334 were adopted by the voters.[26] Perhaps the greatest change to the constitution was the insertion of direct democracy.

DIRECT DEMOCRACY

Railroads and Progressives: The Machine versus the Reformers

Most of the political institutions that dominate California today trace their origins to early twentieth-century Progressive Era reforms. An understanding of the reforms, however, requires knowledge of the practices they sought to change.

---

[24] Constitution of 1849, Article I, Section 2.
[25] California Constitution Article II, Section 1.
[26] California's Constitution from California's Historical Background—California Legislative Counsel, http://www.leginfo.ca.gov/califleg.html.

In the years before the Civil War, the United States launched an era of frantic expansion, fueled by the construction of the national rail network. In 1861, four San Francisco businessmen founded what would become the Southern Pacific Railroad and successfully lobbied Congress to grant them millions of dollars in loan subsidies and land grants. The names of these entrepreneurs—Leland Stanford, Charles Crocker, Mark Hopkins, and Collis Huntington—are still prominent today on buildings, universities, and streets. The railroad made them all incredibly wealthy; Leland Stanford became governor of California.

Economic power usually exists in tandem with political power. The Southern Pacific soon developed a powerful political machine that dominated state politics. The machine controlled the political parties and, working primarily through the dominant Republicans, ensured that its allies held most of the state and local elected offices. These elected officials were naturally expected to protect and advance the interests of their patrons. The railroads and their allies ruled the state, but their success ultimately created the conditions for their demise.

When the railroad coming from California met the Union Pacific line from the east at Promontory Point in Utah in 1869, California became easily accessible to the rest of the nation. Hordes of new people flooded the state and the economy became more diverse through the activities of individuals who did not owe their living to the railroads. An emerging middle class resented the corruption of the railroads' political machine and provided support for the reform movement that eventually emerged.

In 1907, a group of reformers within the Republican Party formed the Lincoln-Roosevelt League. The League, named for Republican presidents Abraham Lincoln and Theodore Roosevelt, was part of the Progressive movement that battled corrupt political machines across the country. Progressive thought emerged at the turn of the century, targeting perceived corruption in the democratic process. Success came quickly, and in 1910 Progressive Republican Hiram Johnson became governor of California.

The Progressives aimed to break the power of the machine and return power to the people. Since the railroads had worked through the political parties, the Progressives directed many of their efforts at giving voters more control over parties and restricting what the parties could do. The direct primary, cross-filing, restrictions on party donations and endorsements, and nonpartisanship in local elections were all intended to weaken the power of the parties (Chapter 3). Since the machine had dominated the legislature and governors, the reformers instituted a system of direct democracy. The initiative, referendum, and recall enabled the voting public to supersede the actions of elected officials and even remove those same officials from office. The Public Utilities Commission (PUC) was created to regulate railroads and utilities, while a new civil service, or merit, system for the hiring and firing of state employees prevented those positions from being used as political favors or pay-offs. In addition to the creation of these political institutions, the Progressives also gave the vote to women, enacted child labor laws, passed workers' compensation laws, and created conservation laws to protect California's natural resources.

In 1911, in an attempt to reduce the influence of parties and elected officials, California became the tenth state to adopt the initiative process, empowering the citizens to adopt laws and constitutional amendments without the support of the government. The Progressives, under the leadership of Governor Hiram Johnson, sought to accomplish the latter through the creation of an elaborate system of direct democracy. In this system, the voters may propose and pass laws and constitutional amendments without input from the governor or legislature (initiative), may overturn laws already passed by the legislature and signed by the governor (referendum), and may remove from office any elected official with whom they are unhappy, even if it is not the end of that person's term (recall). Article II of California's constitution provides for voting, initiative and referendum, and recall.

Indeed, Californians recalled their governor in the fall of 2003, making California only the second state in the nation's history to do so. These tools have been used at both the state and local levels, with the result that the voting public makes some of the most important policy decisions.

The utility of the initiative process became clear during the 1960s constitution revision efforts. By the 1960s, it was evident that the California Constitution needed a facelift. The legislature proposed and the people approved by more than a two-to-one vote Proposition 1a, a constitutional amendment providing for partial or complete revision of the constitution, lifting the restrictions then in place that mandated specific or limited changes to the constitution. The result has been a dramatic overhaul of California's governmental institutions.

Major Features of California's Constitution

A constitution may be considered the "rules of the game" for the game of politics, just as the official rules may determine how the game of basketball is played. A constitution limits the powers of the government; for example, it determines the number of players on the field (e.g. 80 are assembly members and 40 are senators). It provides what each player is allowed to do and what is forbidden; just as basketball players must dribble the ball and are forbidden from simply running down the court with the ball, the legislature is empowered to write laws but must submit bills to the governor first. The things that are forbidden for government and political actors to do often come in the form of protections and rights for the people; as Californians' right to freedom of speech is protected in the constitution, that document simultaneously forbids government actors from encroaching on Californians' rights to free speech. The more complicated the rules, the more complicated the game (after all, it would be a lot easier to play basketball if we COULD simply run down the court with the ball, but that would significantly change how the game is played). California's constitution is quite complex and therefore understanding the "game" of politics is often difficult.

California is governed as a republic but also has features of direct democracy. The California Constitution expressly provides that the powers of government are to be divided into three separate branches: the legislative, the executive, and the judicial. Moreover, the constitution of California is explicit in its articulation of rights,

18

appointments, and removals from office. California's constitution has been amended so many times that a comparison to the federal constitution is insufficient. There are 35 articles in California's constitution, ranging from the establishment of the various institutions of government, to labor relations and medical research. A brief sketch of the constitution follows:

Article I: Article I in California's Constitution contains California's Declaration of Rights. The Declaration of Rights reflects the views that the people are empowered over the government. California's constitution provides for many of the same provisions as the federal Bill of Rights, and it also expands on many of the provisions in the Bill of Rights. The article expressly contains provisions for freedom of religion, speech, the press, the right to petition the government, right to be secure in one's residence, and protections of due process; and Section 1 of the Declaration of Rights acknowledges a specified right to property and privacy: "All people are by nature free and independent and have inalienable rights. Among these are enjoying and defending life and liberty, acquiring, possessing, and protecting property, and pursuing and obtaining safety, happiness, and privacy." In addition, there are provisions that assert the subordination of military power to civil power, prohibitions on discrimination in employment based on sex, race, creed, color, or national or ethnic origin; prohibitions on preferential treatment of persons based on any of these characteristics; and a victims' bill of rights, including financial restitution from the perpetrators of crime and a provision that convicted felons will be "appropriately detained in custody, tried by the courts, and sufficiently punished so that the public safety is protected and encouraged." In addition, California's Declaration of Rights includes many items that would be statutes under federal law, including property owned before or acquired during marriage by gift, will, or inheritance is separate property; the people's right to fish upon and from the public lands of the state and in the waters thereof; and the authorization of the death penalty and provisions that the imposition of the death penalty does not constitute cruel or unusual punishments.

Article II: Article II describes the voting, initiative, referendum, and recall processes for the state. As detailed above, Article II provides for the direct democracy that has enabled the people directly to amend their constitution, make revisions to existing laws, and recall political officials.

Article IV: Article IV defines the structures and powers of the California legislature. It establishes a professional and full-time bicameral legislature that consists of a 40-member senate and an 80-member assembly. In addition, California's legislatures are subject to term limits consisting of three two-year terms for assembly members and two four-year terms for senators. The legislature currently meets in a two-year session under the rules of Proposition 4, adopted in 1972.

Article V: Article V establishes the executive branch, vesting executive power in a single governor to be elected every four years, and it sets the requirements and powers of the governor. However, the California Constitution was quite skeptical of a concentration of powers in executive hands and provided for the separate election of other executive offices, including the lieutenant governor, attorney general, controller, secretary of state, and treasurer. The governor's appointment powers are limited and, like the president's appointment powers, in many cases must be approved by the Senate.

Article VI: Article VI defines the structure, powers, terms, and methods of selection of California's courts. The judicial branch consists of lower trial-level courts called superior courts, each with an appellate division, courts of appeals, and one supreme court, consisting of a chief justice and six associate justices. Furthermore, Article VI provides for a judicial council and to improve the "administration of justice." Judges are elected in nonpartisan elections during general elections: judges of the supreme court are elected at large by the entire state, judges of courts of appeal are elected in their districts, and judges of superior courts are elected in their counties.

Article XVIII: Article XVIII provides for amending California's constitution. The procedures for amending the constitution include both a legislative and a popular method. By a two-thirds vote of each house, the legislature may propose amendments or revisions of the constitution and in the same manner may amend or withdraw its proposal. In addition, the legislature may, by a two-thirds concurring vote, call for a constitutional convention to add amendments or revisions. Finally, through the initiative process, California voters may change the constitution. Regardless of their origin, all changes must be approved by a majority of the electorate voting on the issue. Many of the changes to California's constitution came by way of initiative, including legislative term limits passed in the 1990s to diversify the legislative branch.

Prospects

California's constitution is one of the longest in the world, over 10 times larger than the United States Constitution and in some estimates over 10,000 sheets of paper to print. California's fundamental law has been amended about 500 times by referendum and about 40 times by initiatives since its adoption in 1879. By contrast, the U.S. Constitution has been amended only 27 times in 210 years. The length is largely the result of the initiative process and an electorate that has become increasingly skeptical of government power. Statutory initiatives may be overturned by a majority vote and gubernatorial signature, but a constitutional amendment requires an election to be ratified.

The constitution is not shrinking any time soon. During the 1970s, fewer than 15 initiatives (on average) were filed each year; during the 1980s the filings increased to nearly 30 per year; the 1990s witnessed almost 80 a year. The number of initiatives that actually qualify for the ballot is lower than the number of filings, and those that are approved by the voters are lower still; nevertheless, the increase is impressive. Groups and individuals on all sides of the ideological spectrum are attempting to amend the constitution. However, although the attempts to pass constitutional amendments are continuing, their success has slowed in recent years. In 2005 Governor Schwarzenegger called a special election to consider 8 initiatives—of these, 3 proposed constitutional amendments. Although it is estimated that the special election was the most expensive in California history, none of the initiatives passed, as voters rejected all 8 of the propositions. In November 2006, there were 13 initiatives proposed for voter approval, 5 of which were proposals to amend the constitution; all 5 of the constitutional initiatives failed, and only 7 initiatives passed. In the November 2008 election there were 12 ballot propositions, 3 of which proposed to amend the Constitution. Of these, 2 passed including Proposition 8, a constitutional ban on same sex marriage, and Proposition 9, which would give new rights to crime victims and restrict early release of inmates. The November 2010 General Election ballot did not disappoint with 9 different measures, 5 of which were constitutional amendments, 2 of which intended to change an amendment approved by voters in the most recent preceding election. We will discuss the propositions further in Chapter 4.

While many of the amendments to California's constitution attempt to control corruption and devise an effective governmental structure, others seem to blur the distinction between constitutional law and statutory law. Some of the amendments seem downright silly. For example, amendments to California's constitution have included fee schedules for permits during the three-year phase-out of gill-net fishing. In other words, California's constitution reflects both short-term political passions and a long-term skepticism of government authority.

SOMETHING TO THINK ABOUT

1. How does California's constitution compare with the U.S. Constitution and those of other states in length, detail, structure of governmental powers, and individual rights?

2. How has Californians' skepticism in centralized control of power influenced the state constitution?

3. What specific limits on government are imposed by California's constitution? What future challenges might these restrictions present?

4. How could California meet these challenges?

MULTIPLE-CHOICE QUESTIONS

1) Under the Treaty of Guadalupe Hidalgo,
   a) Mexico ceded California to the U.S.
   b) Americans were given authority to raise the U.S. flag in Monterey in 1846.
   c) Mexico gained independence from Spain.
   d) Mexico declared war on the U.S. in Texas in 1846.
   e) Mexico established a new constitution in 1837.

2) California's first constitution provided for all of the following EXCEPT
   a) separation of powers.
   b) the election of federal officers.
   c) a declaration of rights.
   d) direct democracy.
   e) California's status as a "free" state.

3) The railroads in California
   a) gained considerable power and influence in the state legislature and the political parties.
   b) eventually resulted in amendments to the California Constitution.
   c) led to a flood of new people, diversifying the state and the economy.
   d) helped get Republican members elected to government to advance their cause.
   e) All of the above

4) Article II of California's constitution
   a) was championed by the Republicans in the state legislature to break the power of the railroads and special interests.
   b) was added in 1911 as a result of the corruption of the political parties and the state government to establish the initiative, referendum, and recall.
   c) established a state legislature that was more responsive to the people.
   d) was opposed by the Progressives, who wanted to see greater power in the hands of the people.
   e) made California the first state in the nation to adopt direct democracy.

5) Article I of California's constitution
   a) recognizes a right to property and privacy.
   b) resembles the United States Declaration of Independence.
   c) resembles Article I of the United States Constitution.
   d) includes provisions for affirmative action to demonstrate the state's commitment to civil rights.
   e) is limited to only those things that are contained in the U.S. Bill of Rights.

6) A constitution can be thought of as
   a) a giant bill of rights establishing the rights of the people.
   b) establishing the rules of the game and what political actors must do and what they are forbidden from doing.
   c) suggested guidelines for how to make law.
   d) limits on the people's rights.
   e) a social contract between the government and the governed.

7) California's constitution
   a) has not changed significantly since 1879 when it restructured the assembly and senate.
   b) is roughly equivalent in size and structure to the United States Constitution.
   c) is one of the longest in the world.
   d) A and B only
   e) All of the above

8) All of the following statements about California's direct democracy are true EXCEPT
   a) it is evidenced in the size of the constitution, which has grown considerably since the 1970s.
   b) it has blurred the distinction between constitutional law and statutory law.
   c) it is easily amended and has been amended over 540 times since 1879 through referendum and initiative.
   d) it allows even small items to be included, as California's constitution now contains fee schedules for permits during the three-year phase-out of gill-net fishing.
   e) it forbids voters from amending the constitution.

9) California's constitution may be amended
   a) only by the legislature with a two-thirds vote in each chamber.
   b) only by the legislature with a two-thirds vote in each chamber and with approval from the people.
   c) only by the people in the state of California with a two-thirds vote.
   d) by both the people and the legislature with approval from the governor.
   e) by both the people and the legislature; however, all amendments must be approved by the people.

10) In sum, California's constitution reflects
   a) Californians' complete trust of centralized authority.
   b) California's commitment to government authority over the people to maintain the peace and safety of the people.
   c) Californians' skepticism of centralized authority.
   d) Californians' reluctance to pass constitutional amendments.
   e) California's commitment to affirmative action.

INTERNET SOURCES

State Constitution: **http://www.leginfo.ca.gov/const-toc.html**
California Secretary of State: **http://www.ss.ca.gov**
California's Legislative Council: **http://www.leginfo.ca.gov/**
League of Women Voters: **http://www.lwv.org**

CHAPTER 3: *LOCAL GOVERNMENT*

INTRODUCTION

The basic provisions for the government of California counties and cities are contained in the California Constitution and the California Government Code. A county is the largest political subdivision of the state having corporate powers. The county provides public services, including education, public hospitals, roads maintenance, refuse, and law enforcement. The specific organizational structure of a county in California varies from county to county.

COUNTIES

There are 58 counties in California. They range in population from tiny Alpine, which has 1,208[27] residents, to mighty Los Angeles, whose residents number over 10 million. San Bernardino County, with its 20,164 square miles, is the largest county in the country. There are two types of structures for county governance: general law counties and charter counties.

General Law Counties. General law counties operate under a general set of state laws defining the organization of county government, which includes the number and duties of county-elected officials, as well as an elected county sheriff, an elected district attorney, an elected assessor, and an elected governing body in each county. The legislature has the authority to prescribe uniform procedures for county formation, consolidation, and boundary change.

Charter Counties. Charter counties adopt mini-constitutions called charters. For its own government, a county or city may adopt a charter by majority vote of its electors voting on the question. Charter counties have more autonomy than general law counties, but a charter does not confer upon county officials any extra authority over local regulations, revenue-raising abilities, budgetary decisions, or intergovernmental relations. The state constitution requires that a charter provide for a governing body with a minimum of five or more members, who are elected by district or at large.

There are currently 45 general law counties and 13 charter counties. They are as follows:

General Law Counties: Alpine, Amador, Calaveras, Colusa, Contra Costa, Del Norte, Glenn, Humboldt, Imperial, Inyo, Kern, Kings, Lake, Lassen, Madera, Marin, Mariposa, Mendocino, Merced, Modoc, Mono, Monterey, Napa, Nevada, Plumas, Riverside, San Benito, San Joaquin, San Luis Obispo, Santa Barbara, Santa Cruz, Shasta, Sierra, Siskiyou, Solano, Sonoma, Stanislaus, Sutter, Trinity, Tulare, Tuolumne, Ventura, Yolo, Yuba

---

[27] State of California, Department of Finance, County Population Estimates and Components of Change by County, July 1, 2000-2006. Sacramento, California, April 2010.

Charter Counties: Alameda, Butte, El Dorado, Fresno, Los Angeles, Orange, Placer, Sacramento, San Bernardino, San Diego, San Francisco, San Mateo, Santa Clara, Tehama[28]

Functions

Counties serve three major categories of functions. First, they provide municipal services for the unincorporated parts of the county. Municipal services are generally provided by cities. Services include trash pick-up, local road maintenance, police protection, and fire protection. In the areas of the county that are not parts of cities, county officials provide these services. The sheriff provides law enforcement; county road departments fix roads; vendors hired by the county collect trash; the county fire department answers fire alarms. Sometimes, smaller cities do not have the financial resources to handle all these functions themselves but still wish to incorporate. The problem is normally solved by having cities enter into contracts with the county to provide local services at a set rate for a set fee. These contract cities pay for county personnel to serve their citizens and thus avoid many of the expensive capital costs associated with creating police and fire departments. Lakewood, California pioneered this arrangement in 1955.

The county also provides a number of countywide services that are available to all citizens of the county. The sheriff operates the county jail, while the health department either operates county hospitals or contracts with a vendor to do so. Parks, particularly regional parks, are available throughout the county; county officials inspect restaurants for cleanliness; counties operate systems of dams and channels to protect the public from floods.

Finally, the county serves as the administrator for various programs that are primarily funded by state and local government. The most obvious example is welfare. Welfare policy originates with the federal and state governments, which also provide most of the funding. Anyone wishing to collect a welfare check, however, must go to the county welfare office, which is usually operated by a department of social services.

Government

The Progressives wished to insulate local government from the pernicious influences of party machines, so they made all local elections in California nonpartisan. Since they also wished to maximize public input into the political process, many offices that are appointive in other states are elective in California.

Boards of supervisors govern counties. Generally, these boards are composed of five elected officials who, in the larger counties, serve full-time. Unlike the separation of powers that characterizes the federal and state governments, the board wields both executive and legislative powers. Once elected, the board then elects one of its members to serve as chairman, and also hires a chief administrative officer (CAO) to carry out the directions of the board. Terms for boards of supervisors are four years.

---

[28] 2005 California State Association of Counties.

In progressive California, the people expect to vote for more, not fewer, officials. Thus, while no county except San Francisco elects a mayor, county residents elect a number of other positions. Under state law, county voters must elect a sheriff, a district attorney, and an assessor. The sheriff provides law enforcement and operates the jail; the district attorney is the local prosecutor for all criminal cases in the county; the assessor determines the value of property in the county. The independence of the elected officials often creates interesting challenges for the board of supervisors who create the programs and determine funding levels the elected officials administer.

CITIES

Counties in general are the broad geographic boundaries in which one or more cities are situated, and there are fundamental differences between counties and cities. In general, cities have broader powers of self-government, including authority to raise revenue. Cities are more insulated from legislative control than are the counties. The legislature may delegate functions that belong to the state to the counties unless there are constitutional prohibitions specifically.

If the citizens of an area wish to form their own governmental unit, they may petition to become a city. The petition is considered by the county's local agency formation commission (LAFCO), which determines the fiscal viability of the proposed city. If LAFCO approves, it draws the precise boundaries of the new entity. The board of supervisors then holds hearings and votes. If a majority supports the recommendation, the citizens of the proposed new city vote on whether to incorporate. Like counties, cities may be general law or charter cities; there are 108 charter cities and 370 general law cities.[29]

Functions

Cities serve a wide variety of functions. Primarily, they provide vital municipal services to their residents. Public safety is a top priority. Cities hire chiefs to supervise police departments whose job is to keep the citizens safe. Fire departments battle flames and provide emergency services. Cities also provide streets and street maintenance, parks and recreation, land use planning, utilities, and transportation. As noted above, when the capital investment costs are more than a city can afford, that city may contract with the county or even another city to provide the service.

It is the power to regulate land use that fuels most city incorporation drives. Unincorporated county land uses are regulated by the county supervisors, rulers of a government that, in large urban counties, are often seen as distant, bureaucratic, and unresponsive to local needs.

Government: Council-Manager Cities

Most cities in California have council-manager forms of government. A five-member city council exercises both legislative and executive powers. They hire a professional city

---

[29] League of California Cities 2006.

manager to carry out the council's policies and perform other administrative roles, such as preparing the budget. The council generally elects one of its own members to serve as mayor. That person acts only in a ceremonial role, cutting ribbons and presiding over council meetings. Occasionally these cities will have a directly elected mayor, but that person normally lacks executive powers such as the veto or appointments.

Council-manager cities are based on the theory that policymaking can and should be separate from administration. The council represents the entire city as policymakers, but they are not supposed to be experts. Normally, they serve part-time and are elected at-large (citywide). Administration is the realm of the city manager. Today, the manager may have an advanced degree in public administration and be expected to supervise city departments, but he is expected to follow the policies set by the council. It is never that easy. The manager knows too much to avoid having an influence on policy, while council members sometimes cannot help encroaching on administrative areas. The system, however, is a logical outgrowth of the Progressive reforms early in this century that sought clean, effective government without the domination of political machines.

Government: Mayor-Council Cities

Council-manager governments work best in homogeneous cities where the population is not particularly diverse and where most people generally agree on the role of government. In large, diverse cities, however, a mayor-council form may be more reasonable. These cities have a separation of powers like the federal government and California's state government. The mayor is directly elected and exercises executive powers such as vetoing ordinances (local laws), making appointments of department heads and commission members, and preparing the city budget, which resemble some of the responsibilities of the governor. He or she is expected to represent the voice of the entire city. The council members normally run in separate districts and are expected to represent the interests of their constituents like the members of the state legislature.

Mayor-council cities may have strong or weak mayors depending on how independently the mayor may act. Until recently, Los Angeles was the prototypical weak-mayor city. The mayor of Los Angeles could not even fire the heads of city departments for whose administration he was responsible. In June 1999, however, Los Angeles voters approved a new charter that strengthened the mayor in this and other areas.

Women and minorities. While California has yet to elect a woman governor, its cities have been much friendlier to women and minorities. As of January 2010 there were 68 female mayors in the state of California, 55 of which serve in cities with populations exceeding 30,000; of these, some of the larger cities, including San Bernardino, Sacramento, and Long Beach had elected women as mayors.[30] Several of California's largest cities including San Francisco, Oakland, and Los Angeles have elected minorities for mayor, paving the way for traditionally underrepresented groups to serve in elected office. Currently there are four African American mayors serving in cities with populations exceeding 50,000, including Oakland, Inglewood, Richmond, and

---

[30] U.S. Conference of Mayors, website directory 2010 and personal correspondence

Compton.[31] Antonio Villaraigosa, who was elected in 2005, became the first Latino mayor to serve Los Angeles since 1872, and Santa Ana in Orange County became the first council in the country to have an all-Latino city council following the 2006 general elections in November.

SCHOOL DISTRICTS

There are over 1,000 school districts in California that provide public education for students in grades K–12. These may be elementary or secondary districts or they may be unified districts that educate primary, middle, and high school students.

School districts are governed by elected boards of education. These school board members are normally elected on a nonpartisan, district-wide ballot. They then hire a professional, the superintendent, to administer the programs of the district and carry out the policies of the board.

In the 1990s there was tremendous public dissatisfaction with public schools. Scores on standardized tests had fallen so badly that California ranked at or near the bottom in all national comparisons. These results gave rise to the introduction of an initiative to introduce vouchers in the state. Vouchers would permit any student to use public money to attend any school, public or private. While the initiative was defeated, many educators believed that something had to happen or the next time the proposal would succeed. The answer was charter schools. Today, a school that has the support of a certain number of parents and teachers may request charter status. Private parties also may ask to start a charter school. While funds still reach the school through the district, the charter school is freed of many of the state and local regulations that limit what it can do. Currently, there are several hundred charter schools in California. It is too early to assess their success, but some have experienced financial difficulties or curricular controversies.

SPECIAL DISTRICTS

Special districts provide narrow, specialized services to a limited geographic area. Either local residents or local government may request the creation of such a district. LAFCO then acts as it does on requests for incorporation, followed by a popular vote. Most of these districts are independent, with their own elected governing boards. Some are dependent on another level of government, usually the county. In that case, the district's governing board is the board of supervisors.

The range of services provided by special districts is staggering. There are water districts, flood control districts, hospital districts, and cemetery districts. Residents can form lighting districts to pay for the installation of streetlights, or vector control districts to control rats and mosquitoes. Their funding may come from local property taxes, benefit assessments, or special fees.

---

[31] National Conference of Black Mayors, April 2007.

SECESSION

Although Los Angeles voters voted against San Fernando Valley and Hollywood secession proposals in November 2002, the secessionist movement helped reshape California law and shake up the nation's second-largest city. Valley secessionists rewrote state law to allow voters, over city councils, to decide the fate of cityhood proposals. To do so, they collected signatures from 25 percent of the Valley's registered voters, triggering a study of the secession's financial effects and forcing Los Angeles leaders to take their complaints ever more seriously. Although on Election Day the proposal was supported by residents in the Valley, Hollywood residents rejected the measure, and the greater Los Angeles community overwhelmingly rejected both proposals. Then-mayor James K. Hahn led the antisecession campaign, recruiting municipal unions, black and Latino leaders, billionaire business moguls, and most of the city's politicians to raise money to put down the Valley and Hollywood insurrections. Over $7 million was spent to counteract the secessionist proposal, more than four times the secessionists' $1.7 million.

Despite losing the vote, secessionists' grassroots crusade for more local control did realize some success and helped focus public debate on their complaints that City Hall is wasteful, arrogant, and unresponsive. During the 1999 overhaul of the City Charter, many secessionists pressed for a system of neighborhood councils empowered with land use and budget authority. Instead, the councils wound up being advisory panels, which convinced many residents that breaking off from Los Angeles was the only solution. Mayor Hahn vowed to keep the city together and to meet the demands of the Valley residents who felt that their needs were not being met.

DEMOCRACY AT WORK: INCORPORATION IN MALIBU

Unincorporated areas may wish to become cities for many reasons, such as land-use planning. In the case of Malibu, however, the purpose was to prevent the county from forcing the residents to accept and pay for sewers.

Malibu is a beautiful part of northern Los Angeles County. It is an area where rugged mountains meet the Pacific Ocean. It also is a land of continuing disaster since the ground is very unstable and slides are frequent. Fires are also constant visitors, so Malibu seems to face a recurring cycle of fires in the summer that denude the land and make way for floods and landslides in the winter. Residents, including many in the film industry, have rebuilt a number of times.

Generally, Malibu residents are antigrowth. They feel that development will spoil the pristine rural atmosphere of the place. Most of the houses have septic tanks to receive their waste, and proposals for modernizing the system with sewers is viewed as an invitation to expanded development.

In the late 1980s, the county moved to put sewers in Malibu. County officials had become convinced that the septic tanks were leaking and potentially contributing to landslides in the area. Furthermore, tests of bacteria counts on streets and even sidewalks after storms indicated a potential health hazard. The county proposed to install sewer lines that would be financed by the residents. While the cost would be spread over 20 years, it would still be considerable. The county, however, was insistent, since it did not want to be held liable in suits that might arise over the situation.

The answer of the Malibu majority was to incorporate. A combination of those who did not want to bear the costs and those who were convinced it was a plot to open the hills to development carried the day. In the end, the issue was one of land-use determination, but Malibu is still widely known as the city that came into being to avoid having sewers.

SOMETHING TO THINK ABOUT

1. How has California's Progressive thought influenced local governance?

2. What are the advantages and disadvantages in having a council-manager city versus a mayor-council city?

3. What are the costs and opportunities for charter counties over general law counties?

4. What types of challenges face California's educational system? How have charter schools played a role in shaping the future of California's education system?

5. What are the advantages and disadvantages for cities to incorporate?

MULTIPLE-CHOICE QUESTIONS

1) The two types of structures for county governance are
   a) general law and municipal.
   b) municipal and council-manager.
   c) unincorporated and general law.
   d) incorporated and municipal.
   e) general law and charter.

2) General law counties
   a) operate under a general set of state laws defining the organization of county government.
   b) adopt mini-constitutions called charters.
   c) make up the smallest percentage of counties in California.
   d) All of the above
   e) None of the above

3) Counties generally
    a) offer park services to county residents.
    b) operate the jails under the supervision of the sheriff.
    c) operate the hospitals and inspections for health.
    d) administer welfare.
    e) All of the above

4) The Progressive spirit is evident in local government in that
    a) some counties choose their own local government.
    b) local elections are nonpartisan and include many different kinds of offices.
    c) the state runs the elections in the counties.
    d) the counties are responsible for distributing welfare.
    e) the counties all institute term limits in all offices.

5) The governing structure of a county is called the
    a) mayor-council.
    b) board of supervisors.
    c) charter.
    d) assessor.
    e) None of the above

6) The function of a city includes all of the following EXCEPT
    a) operating the jail.
    b) police and fire department.
    c) regulation of land use.
    d) street maintenance.
    e) utilities.

7) Cities that are more homogenous use a _____ form of government that
   _____.
    a) council-manager; exercises both legislative and executive powers
    b) municipal; separates the powers of the legislative and executive
    c) charter; exercises only legislative powers
    d) general law; exercises only executive powers
    e) mayor-council; separates the powers of government

8) Which type of city governance closely resembles the federal and state governments due to its separation of powers?
    a) Council-manager
    b) Charter
    c) Municipal
    d) Mayor-council
    e) General law

9) School districts
   a) must be either elementary or secondary districts.
   b) may be unified districts that educate primary, middle, and high school students.
   c) are governed by an elected board of education and an elected superintendent.
   d) are governed by a state appointed board of education and an elected superintendent.
   e) hire professionals to run the board.

10) Inhabitants of unincorporated areas generally wish to incorporate because
   a) they could refuse to accept and pay for certain services, including sewers.
   b) they could rely on the county for municipal services.
   c) they could fight new development.
   d) fewer people would want to move into the area.
   e) A and C only

INTERNET SOURCES

Association of Bay Area Governments: **http://www.abag.ca.gov/**
Southern California Association of Governments: **http://www.scag.ca.gov/**
San Diego Association of Governments: **http://www.sandag.cog.ca.us/**
League of California Cities: **http://cacities.org**
California Association of Counties: **http://www.csac.counties.org/default.asp?id=7**
Individual cities and counties also have their own sites. For example, Los Angeles County's is: **http://lacounty.info/**
Special districts have their own sites. The site for the Metropolitan Transit Authority in Los Angeles County is: **http://mta.net**

CHAPTER 4: *POLITICAL PARTICIPATION IN CALIFORNIA*

INTRODUCTION

Californians vote on a tremendous number of items. General elections occur every two years and may include any and all of the following: the governor, other statewide executives, judges of California's Supreme and Appellate courts, members of the U.S. Senate, members of the U.S. House of Representatives, local government officials including county boards of supervisors, county judges, city council, mayor, in addition to electors of the Electoral College. They also vote on numerous propositions resulting from initiatives and referenda at both the state and local levels.

VOTER QUALIFICATIONS

The qualifications to vote in California are established in Article II of the California Constitution. To be eligible to vote, a person must be a United States citizen and a resident of California; at least 18 years of age (or will be by the date of the next election); and registered to vote. Registering to vote is fairly simple and interested voters can download a form from the Secretary of State's Web page, or find a registration card at a variety of public offices. In addition, in 1993, Congress passed The National Voter Registration Act, also known as the Motor Voter law, which permits people conducting business at a DMV office to register to vote or update their voter registration information. A 1985 Court of Appeal decision held that a homeless person may register to vote at "a location deemed by the voter to be a dwelling place or place of habitation for that voter, but must provide a mailing address in order to receive election materials. Those people serving time in prison or on parole for a commission of a felony or judged by a court to be mentally incompetent are ineligible to vote. However, those people who are in a local jail as a result of a misdemeanor conviction; are awaiting trial or are currently on trial and have not yet been convicted of a crime; have completed parole for a felony conviction; or are on probation may register to vote. To register to vote, the registration form must be signed, dated, and postmarked at least 15 days before the date of election. In addition, voters may choose to cast an absentee ballot if they expect to be away or do not wish to go to the polls on the day of the election.

In 2006, a federal and state law went into effect mandating that interested voters who register to vote must provide identification when they register to vote, if they have it. If they do not have a driver's license or state identification card number, or a Social Security number, they can still register to vote. After confirming that the applicant does not have either a driver's license or state identification card number or a Social Security number, the county elections office will assign a unique identification number to the voter.[32]

According to the September 3, 2010 Report of Voter Registration produced by the secretary of state, voter registration was 72.24 percent of eligible voters or 16,993,075 voters. This represents a decrease from 2008's high of 17,304,091 in the last presidential

---

[32] For more information please go to: http://www.sos.ca.gov/elections/guidetovr_1006.pdf

election. As Figure 4:1 depicts, the percent of eligible voters who have registered has hovered around 70 percent, so this number is not unusual.

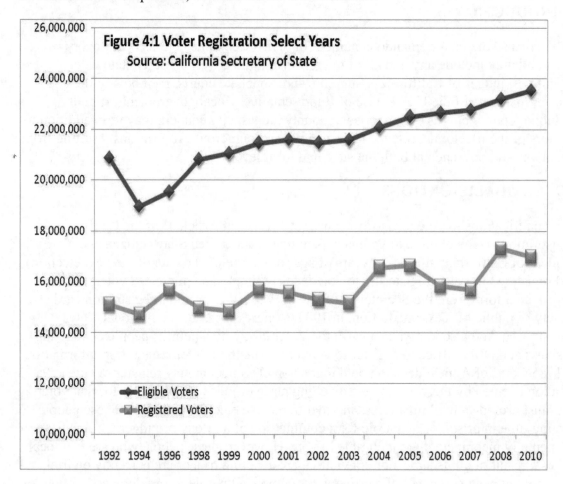

In the 2000 presidential elections, the state of Florida experienced a host of problems with its voting equipment, raising questions regarding the validity of votes that were cast. During the recount, many votes were never counted because of time constraints. As a response, Californians passed Proposition 43 during the 2002 primary elections, which included the following language into Article II: "A voter who casts a vote in an election in accordance with the laws of this State shall have that vote counted."[33]

ELECTIONS IN CALIFORNIA

Types of Elections

In even-numbered years, there are actually two statewide elections in California. The general election in November allows the voters to choose from among the candidates of the political parties for various offices. The candidates are presented in an office block ballot, which means they are listed by the office sought. These candidates are the nominees of their parties and were chosen earlier in the year in a primary election.

---

[33] Section 2.5, Article II, California Constitution.

California's Primary Elections

Historically, California operated a closed primary, which meant that only citizens registered with a particular political party could vote to select that party's nominees. In 1996, however, Proposition 198, a popular initiative, changed that system to an open, or blanket, primary. Under the blanket primary, every registered voter received the same ballot, except for county central committees. This meant that voters could vote for a Democrat for governor and a Republican for lieutenant governor and a Green Party candidate for state assembly, all on the same ballot and regardless of the voter's own political party affiliation.

Some interesting results ensued, following the implementation of the blanket primary. In 2000, Independents and Democrats were credited for nominating Orange County's 72nd Assembly Republican candidate. While Bruce Matthias had the support of the Republican Party and won more Republican votes than any other candidate in the primary, Matthias lost to fellow Republican Lynn Daucher. Daucher, who was considered more moderate than Matthias, attracted votes from non-Republicans, many of them Democrats, to win a six-point primary victory over Matthias.[34]

The open primary deeply concerned the major political parties. Both Democrats and Republicans feared that voters from other parties would interfere with their nominations and perhaps select weaker rather than stronger candidates. The two parties, therefore, successfully challenged the open primary law in federal court. On June 26, 2000, the United States Supreme Court issued a decision in *California Democratic Party* v. *Jones*, stating that California's "open" primary system, established by Proposition 198, was unconstitutional because it violated a political party's First Amendment right of association.

The result of the decision is a "modified" closed primary system. The new system took effect on January 1, 2001, and permits unaffiliated ("decline to state") voters to participate in a primary election if authorized by an individual party's rules. The first primary under these new rules was held in March 2002, and the American Independent Party, the Democratic Party, and the Republican Party all agreed to the rules of the modified closed primary. However, this is not the end of California's experimentation with primary election schemes, as voters approved a legislative constitutional initiative on the June 2010 primary election ballot again changing the way Californians select their nominees. The measure resembles an open primary, requiring that candidates run in a single primary open to all registered voters, with the top two vote-getters meeting in a runoff. The new system will take effect in the 2012 elections. The constitutionality of the measure is in question however, as it was challenged in July 2010 and awaiting a decision.

---

[34] Ellis, John 2000. "Parties Fear For Voting Power: Top Court Will Decide if Prop. 198 Robs Groups of The Ability To Select Their Own Nominee," *Fresno Bee* A1 April 23, 2000.

Presidential Delegate Selection

The Democratic and Republican national parties select their candidates for president in a presidential nominating convention. Each party in each state chooses its delegates to this convention. California's parties have traditionally selected their delegates using the statewide primary in presidential election years.

Traditionally, California held its primary on the first Tuesday after the first Monday in June. This date, however, put the state at a significant disadvantage in the competition to influence the selection of presidential nominees. Since caucuses and primaries in other states begin in early February, the nomination usually was decided before the campaign even reached California. The last time the Democratic primary affected the outcome at the convention was in 1972 when George McGovern won. Republican primary votes were last decisive in 1964 when Barry Goldwater defeated Nelson Rockefeller. In an effort to increase California's influence, the state held its 1996 primaries in late March. California still was not significant, however, since most of the delegates to both conventions were already selected by that date. This was deeply troubling to the parties, who reasoned that California should be a significant determinant in the primary elections, given that both parties operate a winner-take-all system whereby the GOP candidate with the most primary votes picks up all 162 of 1,034 total delegate votes and the Democrat takes all 433 of 4,337 total votes. In 2000, therefore, the state moved its primary to the first Tuesday after the first Monday in March. However, in 2005 the legislature enacted Senate Bill 1730, changing California's primary elections back to June. The story does not end here. California's legislature moved the primary date for the presidential election back yet again. For the 2008 presidential primary, the primary election was held Tuesday, February 5, 2008, but the remaining primaries were held in June as passed by state law in 2005.

The effects of this change are unclear. While California received more attention from the presidential primary candidates in the season leading up to the primary election, many other states moved their primary dates as well and held them on Super Tuesday on February 5 like California. Another consideration is the effect the split primaries had on voter turnout. As it is, fewer voters turn out for the primaries than the general election, as depicted in Figure 4:2. In 2008 voters were asked to participate in February for the presidential primary and seven initiatives that qualified for the February ballot but also were asked to show up in June for the primary elections for their assembly members and House members, and their state senator if he or she was up for reelection in the fall in addition to two initiatives. While voter turnout in the February 5 primary set an all-time high record, the June 2008 primary was an all-time low for California.

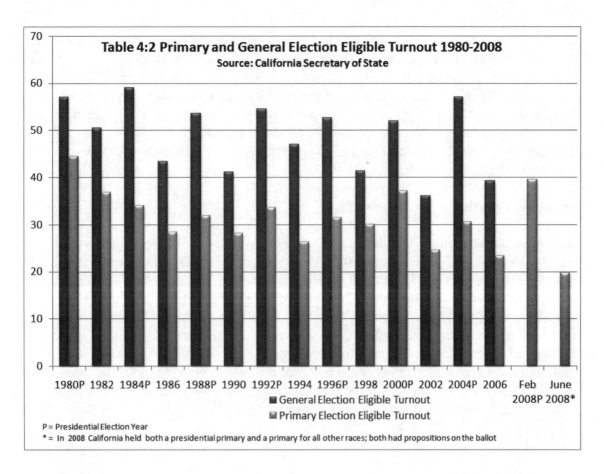

Table 4:2 Primary and General Election Eligible Turnout 1980-2008
Source: California Secretary of State

■ General Election Eligible Turnout
▨ Primary Election Eligible Turnout

P = Presidential Election Year
* = In 2008 California held both a presidential primary and a primary for all other races; both had propositions on the ballot

Special Elections

In addition to statewide primary and general elections, California also holds special elections from time to time. The governor calls these elections. He or she has the right to call one whenever he or she wishes to place outstanding issues on the ballot. The governor also must call them in certain circumstances, including recalls and replacements for state legislative and congressional seats which become vacant more than 180 days before the next general election. This does not apply to vacancies in the U.S. Senate, which are filled by gubernatorial nomination. The most recent state-wide special election held November 8, 2005, was called by the governor to address eight statutory and constitutional initiatives. The election, which cost the state millions of dollars, was a failure for those advocates of the initiatives, which included the governor's personal agenda. One of the initiatives set out to amend the procedure for redistricting California's senate, assembly, congressional, and Board of Equalization districts. All eight initiatives were rejected.

Turnout

As Figure 4:2 depicts, California's turnout steadily decreased from 1972 until 1994, although clearly more Californians turn out to vote in a presidential year than the midterm election. This may be troubling, as California elects its governor during the midterm elections, but like most states across the country, the largest turnout is typically for the presidential general elections. Also notice that the percentage of voters who turn out during the primaries is considerably lower in every election year than the percentage of voters who turn out in a general election. Primary voters are usually more involved and more politically aware than those who do not vote in the primaries; moreover, primary voters tend to be more loyal to their party than nonprimary voters. Since the number of voters who are willing to register with a political party is shrinking, primary elections may continue to suffer from poor turnout. In November 2008, 12,472,507 voters participated in the vote for president and the election had record numbers of voters registered to vote.

Voting for President

Electors gather on the first Monday after the second Wednesday in December (most recently, December 15, 2008) to cast their votes. Since Barack Obama won the state handily—60.9 percent to 37.3 percent for Republican John McCain—the Democrat electors assembled in the Assembly Chambers of the State Capitol at 2:00 p.m. to cast their votes, voting separate ballots for President and Vice President. The results are sealed and delivered to the Secretary of the United States Senate for transmittal to the President of the Senate; the Senate tallies the states' votes and officially declares the result to the President. Electors are paid $10 plus mileage (5¢ per mile) for the round trip from their homes to the Capitol for the meeting of the Electoral College. Arrangements for the meeting are handled through the Governor's office.[35]

INITIATIVE

California is one of 24 states where anyone with an idea and enough signatures on petitions can take laws and constitutional amendments to the voters for their approval or rejection. The initiative is a procedure by which the people may propose and pass laws and constitutional amendments. The procedure begins with interested citizens drafting a proposal. These citizens may be elected officials; governors and legislators use the technique to bypass the legislature to appeal directly to the voters. Interest groups also frequently sponsor initiatives, and occasionally wealthy individuals propose initiatives. The proposal, along with $200, is sent to the attorney general, who prepares a summary of and title for the measure. The secretary of state actually gives the permission to circulate petitions after assigning deadlines for the submission of signatures. Only registered voters at the time of signing are entitled to sign a petition, and the petition must be circulated in their county of registration.

The Progressives who created the initiative did not wish to overwhelm the voting public with every idea Californians might have. Therefore, they established a requirement that the proponents must obtain the signatures of other registered voters to insure somewhat broad support. There are two kinds of initiatives. For a statewide constitutional amendment initiative, the number of signatures must equal 8 percent of the total votes cast for all candidates for governor the last time that official was elected. To qualify for circulation before the 2010 election cycle, proponents needed 694,354 signatures for a constitutional amendment. For a statutory initiative, which has the force of law but is

---

[35] http://www.sos.ca.gov/elections/sov/2004_general/sov_pref14_15_electing_pres.pdf

overridden by any conflicting provisions in the state constitution, the number is 5 percent of the total vote for governor, currently 433,971 signatures. The proponents have 150 days to collect the signatures, which are then certified by the secretary of state's office, working with local county registrars of voters. A proposal with enough valid signatures then appears on the next statewide ballot occurring 131 days or more after the measure has been declared qualified. If a special election occurs after the 131 days but before a general election, the initiative will appear on that ballot. It takes a majority of those voting to approve a measure. If two conflicting proposals are approved at the same election, the one with the larger "yes" vote becomes law. The approved initiative takes effect immediately following the election and does not need the approval of the governor (nor can the governor veto an initiative) or the legislature. Furthermore, the initiative may not be amended or repealed by the legislature.

REFERENDUM

Referenda give voters the power to overturn laws already passed by the legislature and signed by the governor as well as an opportunity to approve constitutional amendments, bond issues, and other laws proposed to them by the legislature. The protest referendum permits voters to overturn enacted laws. The referendum may not apply to bills that are designated as urgent by a two-thirds vote of both houses of the legislature, bills calling elections, or bills that either impose taxes or spend money (appropriations bills). Those items are so vital that the system does not permit delay to await a popular vote. For all other laws, however, proponents have 90 days to collect a number of signatures of registered voters equal to 5 percent of the total vote for governor. The number of days is a significant barrier, since advocates must collect the same number of signatures required for statutory initiatives but in only slightly more than half the time. Protest referenda, therefore, rarely qualify. Compared to initiatives, referenda are invoked infrequently. Since 1912, there have been approximately 50 attempts to qualify referenda for the ballot. Of the 50 attempts, 39 qualified for the ballot, 25 of which were approved by voters.

Compulsory referenda, however, appear on most statewide ballots. The Progressives wanted the people to have input on certain major decisions. Therefore, all amendments to the state constitution approved by the legislature and the governor as well as state general obligation bond measures must be referred to the people for approval. The legislature also has the option of referring to the people other legislation for enactment. These are optional referenda.

The fourth type of referendum is referred to as an advisory referendum. This is an expression of the opinions of the people. Although these referenda have no legal standing, they are a method of communicating voters' desires to their elected representatives. These votes tend to occur more at the local level when city councils ask their constituents for their opinions on certain controversial items. In the last few years, for example, cities in California have asked the opinions of voters on matters such as whether a city should impose a utility tax to help pay its bills and whether a city should merge its fire department with the county fire department.

Direct Democracy: A Closer Look

The initiative process was intended to give the people the power to propose laws. Formidable barriers, however, make it unrealistic for an average citizen to be a successful advocate. The collection of hundreds of thousands of valid signatures of registered voters in 150 days is difficult and expensive. Usually, it is accomplished through funding elaborate mailings or hiring professional signature-gathering firms. Typically, this costs one to two million dollars; therefore, wealthy individuals or groups have an advantage in realizing success. These may be groups or individuals advancing ideas they think are right, politicians seeking to enhance their reputations, or others who stand to benefit if the law is enacted.

Staging the special election in 2005 cost taxpayers over $50 million, while unions, business donors, and other contributors spent an additional $250 million. Proposition 75 was the most expensive battle waged during the 2005 special election. The initiative would have forced public employee labor organizations to obtain the prior consent of every member before using dues or fees for political contributions, severely dampening the employee unions' ability to raise campaign money. The advocates for the initiative spent about $4.6 million, while those opposed raised $41.8 million. Additionally, Governor Schwarzenegger's initiative committees promoting Propositions 74, 75, 76, and 77 raised $50 million.

It is important to note that even a successful initiative still faces challenges. The most obvious barrier is the court system, which from time to time determines that the initiative violates state or federal constitutional provisions or conflicts with federal law. Constitutions override statutes, and federal law prevails in conflicts with state law. Following the 2008 general election, California is once again embroiled in a court battle over one of its initiatives. Perhaps one of the most contentious issues to reach California and the nation is the issue of same-sex marriage. In 2000, Californians passed Proposition 22, also known as the Knight Initiative after its main proponent, with 61 percent support; the proposition mandated that only marriages between a man and woman are valid in California. However, in May 2008, California's Supreme Court struck down the state's ban on same-sex marriage by a 4–3 vote. Chief Justice Ronald M. George writing for the majority opinion declared that the state Constitution protects a fundamental "right to marry" that extends equally to same-sex couples; furthermore he continued, "any law that discriminates on the basis of sexual orientation will from this point on be constitutionally suspect in California in the same way as laws that discriminate by race or gender."[36] Governor Schwarzenegger responded by saying he "respects" the decision and would "not support an amendment to the constitution that would overturn" it. Since the ruling, there have been more than 18,000 same-sex weddings in California, which began in June 2008.

Opponents of same-sex marriage responded immediately, collecting signatures for a referendum known as Proposition 8 to ban same sex marriage under California's Constitution. On November 4, 2008, Proposition 8 passed with 52 percent of the vote and

---

[36] Dolan, Maura May 18, 2008, "California Supreme Court overturns gay marriage ban" *Los Angeles Times*

42

more than $70 million spent on advertising by both sides, a new record for a social policy initiative. The California Supreme heard challenges to Proposition 8 under Constitutional procedural grounds and held that the proposition had been passed constitutionally. However, the Court's ruling did not settle the question of gay marriage in California; instead it merely continued an ongoing state and national debate that both the courts and the voters will again play a large role in deciding. In August 2010 a federal district court struck down the law under the Equal Protection Clause of the U.S. Constitution's Fourteenth Amendment. However, just weeks later the Ninth Federal Circuit Court stayed the district court ruling to allow the proponents of the ban to organize an appeal.

A note about initiatives in California should include the questionable constitutional nature of California's statutes. In November 2010 voters will decide whether to enact a statute that would legalize marijuana for people 21 and over to possess, cultivate or transport for personal use. The federal government has already indicated it will challenge the law if it passes. The Supreme Court declared on two different occasions that California's compassionate use act, passed by voters in 1996, violated federal law.

Figures 4:3 and 4:4 show the increases in initiatives over time. In the last 20 years, the use of the initiative in California has exploded. Between 1976 and 1996, there were 106 statewide ballot initiatives, compared to only 29 in the 20 years preceding.[37] According to the Public Policy Institute of California, there have been 107 ballot initiatives in this decade alone, including those on the November 4 ballot. Despite the increasing numbers of initiatives that are proposed and eventually qualify for balloting, barely one-third of them are approved by the voters. Figure 4:3 illustrates the increase in ballot initiatives over time and their varying success rates. Each primary and general election includes at least one important or controversial proposal. In the last few years, the public has been asked to vote on issues such as abolishing bilingual education in public schools; prohibiting racial preference or discrimination in public education, employment, or contracting; approving casino gambling on tribal lands; and prohibiting same-sex couples from marrying.

---

[37] Gerber, Elisabeth, 1998. *Interest Group Influence in the California Initiative Process*, Public Policy Institute of California.

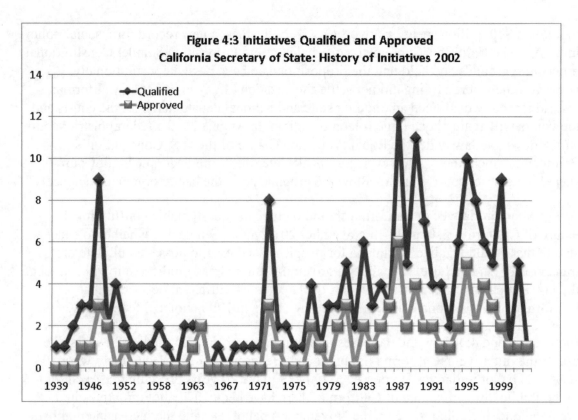

Figure 4:3 Initiatives Qualified and Approved
California Secretary of State: History of Initiatives 2002

According to the Public Policy Institute of California, 60 percent of Californians and likely voters say the public policy decisions made by voters through the initiative process are probably better than those made by the governor and legislature. However, six out of ten voters also say California asks them to vote on too many initiatives.[38]

Coupled with the sheer number of initiatives is the increase in spending. Average per-measure spending increased from $3 million in 1976 to over $8 million in 1996.[39]

---

[38] "Californians and the Initiative Process" Just the Facts, PPIC November 2008
[39] Gerber, Elisabeth, 1998. *Interest Group Influence in the California Initiative Process*, Public Policy Institute of California.

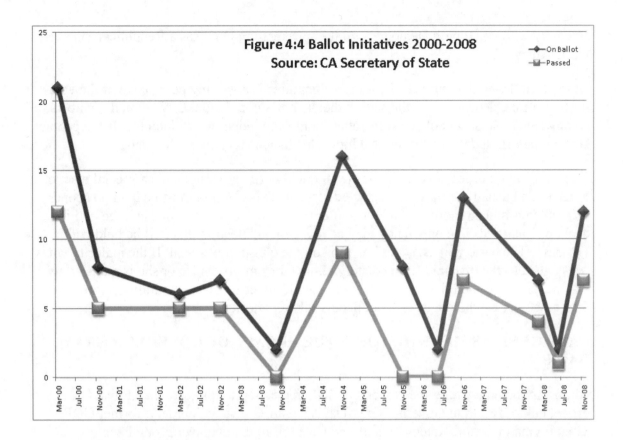

Figure 4:4 Ballot Initiatives 2000-2008
Source: CA Secretary of State

As Californians strongly disapprove of their state leaders today, preference for initiatives over the governor or legislature has increased somewhat since 2006. Three in four residents would favor a system of review and revision of initiatives to avoid legal issues and drafting errors. Seventy-seven percent favor an increase in public disclosure of funding for signature-gathering and initiative campaigns. [40]

RECALL

Elected officials serve terms of predetermined length, generally four years. The Progressives believed, however, that the people should be able to remove officials early if the voters are unhappy with their performances. If citizens wish to remove a statewide elected official, they must circulate a petition to indicate enough support to make it worthwhile to put the item on the ballot. The petition contains the reason for the suggested recall as well as a rebuttal from the targeted official. No one, however, judges the sufficiency of either statement. For statewide officials such as the governor, the number of signatures collected within 160 days must equal 12 percent of the total vote for all candidates for that office the last time an election was held, currently 897,158. In more than 31 attempts spanning a century, the recall of a California governor had never made it from the petition phase to reality until 2003.

For recall of state legislators, the number of required signatures must equal 20 percent of the total vote for that office in the last election. While rare, these recalls do occur. In 1995, the Republican Party engineered the recall of two of its own members of the

45

assembly who voted with Democrats on the speakership. One was a Republican speaker, Doris Allen.

At the local level, the number of required signatures is a varying percentage of the vote for that office, depending on the size of the district's population. City council members, county supervisors, school board members, and even judges are vulnerable. If the people elected the official, they may remove him. This happens relatively frequently.

Once a recall qualifies, an election follows quickly. The governor calls a special election to recall and usually replaces the targeted official. This election must be held no sooner than 60 days and no more than 80 days after the signatures are verified and the petition declared qualified. The only delay may be to a general election that will be held within 180 days. The basic vote is a "yes" or "no" on the question of recall. If the majority votes "yes," the elected official is immediately removed from office. He or she is replaced by whichever of the candidates running to succeed him/her receives a plurality (more votes than any other candidate, though not necessarily a majority).

CALIFORNIANS MAKE HISTORY: THE RECALL OF GOVERNOR GRAY DAVIS

Almost immediately after the November 2002 reelection to his second and final term of office, talk of recalling Governor Gray Davis began. By early February, former GOP assemblyman Howard Kaloogian and Ted Costa from the taxpayer group People's Advocate, formally launched campaigns to place a recall election against the governor on a special ballot.

U.S. Representative Darrell Issa (R-Vista) bankrolled the petition drive to put the recall on the ballot, underwriting the recall drive with $1.7 million and pledging to announce his candidacy for governor should the recall drive prove successful. By mid-July, Secretary of State Kevin Shelly had certified over 1.3 million signatures, and Lieutenant Governor Cruz Bustamante set California's first gubernatorial recall election for October 7. The ballot would pose two questions to voters: First: Should the governor keep his job? Second: Who should replace him if he is removed from office?

The weeks ensuing were anything but "politics as usual" for California. Perhaps punctuated most dramatically by movie star Arnold Schwarzenegger's announcement that he would run on *The Tonight Show with Jay Leno*, the ballot listed 135 candidates who had paid their $3,500 fees, gathered their 60 signatures, and filed at local registrars' offices by the August 9 deadline. In the end, Issa dropped out after spending $2.96 million. Included in the unusual list of candidates were Republicans State Senator Tom McClintock (R-Thousand Oaks); multimillionaire businessman Bill Simon, Jr., who had lost to Davis in the November election; and multimillionaire Peter Ueberroth, the former commissioner of Major League Baseball and head of Los Angeles's 1984 Olympic games. Democratic Party leaders at the national level vowed to defeat the recall and stay out of the replacement race, fearing that offering another choice would erode the governor's support. But California Democrats, increasingly concerned about Davis's vulnerability, moved to recruit an alternative candidate. When Senator Dianne Feinstein declined to enter the race, Lieutenant Governor Cruz Bustamante stepped forward. In addition, a host of others, including Gary Coleman, former child actor; adult film actress Mary "Carey" Cook; pornographer Larry Flynt; and, running as an independent, political commentator Arianna Huffington entered the race. By the time of the election, the field of competitive players had narrowed; Ueberroth and Simon as well as Huffington had dropped out.

In the meantime, Governor Davis and his supporters' efforts to thwart the recall proved unsuccessful, as challenges to the recall in state court were rejected. The first challenge sought to delay the election until March because the use of punch-card ballots and the consolidation of polling places could potentially deny voters in some counties their equal protection right to have their votes count as much as others. A second petition sought to allow the governor to be a candidate to succeed himself, claiming that his absence violates the equal protection rights of his supporters. The final petition claimed that California's recall process violates the federal constitutional guarantee of a republican form of government by frustrating majority rule, since the governor could be removed by only slightly more than 50 percent of those voting while a successor could be elected with a much smaller percentage of the votes.

While Davis was not a party to federal suits, a month later a three-judge panel of the Ninth Circuit Court of Appeals ordered the election postponed, agreeing with the American Civil Liberties Union that punch-card machines used in counties that included more than 40 percent of registered voters would unfairly disenfranchise people because of the machines' error rate. The decision was immediately appealed by the state and representatives from prorecall factions. A week later, a larger panel of the same appeals court unanimously reversed the earlier decision.

Over 55 percent of voters agreed that the governor should be recalled, handing the governorship over to political neophyte Arnold Schwarzenegger, who won 48.6 percent of the votes cast. In the end, voter turnout proved to be the highest in a nonpresidential election year since 1982, as 60 percent of registered voters (approximately 9.25 million) participated in the election, far higher than the 50 percent who took part in the November 2002 gubernatorial election.

Many proponents applaud the process, claiming that the recall of Governor Davis proves that democracy works, and that the people are capable of speaking their minds and asserting their place in California governance. However, those who opposed the recall argue that the Davis recall will set a dangerous precedent, as the recall thwarts the democratic process by undermining the votes cast in earlier elections.

SOMETHING TO THINK ABOUT

1. How has California's Progressive tradition impacted its voter participation?

2. What are the effects of the Progressive reforms on special interest participation in California?

3. Has direct democracy achieved its intended effects?

4. Despite the number of initiatives proposed in any given election cycle, few pass, and those that do may not be amended by the legislature but only by another initiative; furthermore, initiatives are subject to court override. What does the fact that initiatives are frequently the subject of litigation suggest in terms of the people's ability to write law?

5. Is the low voter turnout in California a problem? If so, how can California remedy the situation?

MULTIPLE-CHOICE QUESTIONS

1) Voters in California are likely to vote in which of the following elections?
   a) Congressional
   b) State senatorial
   c) Assembly
   d) Initiative
   e) All of the above

2) The qualifications for voting in California include all of the following except
   a) minimum age of 18.
   b) California state residency.
   c) United States citizenship.
   d) English literacy.
   e) voter registration.

3) In response to the failure to count each and every ballot in the state of Florida during the 2000 presidential election recount,
   a) Californians passed an initiative declaring that all votes cast in an election be counted.
   b) the governor passed an initiative declaring that all votes cast in an election be counted.
   c) the state legislature passed a law declaring that all votes cast in an election be counted.
   d) the governor vetoed an initiative passed by Californians demanding that all votes cast in an election be counted.
   e) Californians passed a referendum that mandated all voting machines must be regulated by the state so that all votes cast in an election be counted.

4) California's primary elections are currently
   a) blanket primaries, whereby only party members are eligible to participate in the party's primary.
   b) closed primaries, whereby only party members are eligible to participate in the party's primary.
   c) modified closed primaries, in which those who decline to state a party can select any of the party's ballots provided those parties agree.
   d) blanket primaries, whereby any registered voter can participate in the primaries and can select a candidate from any party for any office.
   e) None of the above

5) The presidential delegate selection in California
   a) has occurred on the same day every four years since 1964.
   b) has occurred on a variety of days every four years since 1996.
   c) has only occurred once, in 1972, when George McGovern won.
   d) is a source of tension because Californians, as residents of the largest state, wish to have more influence in the outcome of the selection process.
   e) B and D only

6) The 2008 presidential primary and delegate selection created which situation?
   a) There were always too many primary voters and not enough general election voters.
   b) California probably asked too much of its voters by adding yet another election, making the June 2008 primary the lowest turnout on record.
   c) Voters could not find any information on the candidates and were therefore not able to vote.
   d) Primary voters tend to be less politically knowledgeable than general election voters.
   e) All of the above

7) An initiative
   a) may be amended by the governor.
   b) is a measure passed by the legislature and presented to the voters for approval.
   c) may be amended by the state legislature.
   d) is a measure written by the voters and presented to the voters for approval.
   e) is relatively easy and inexpensive to have placed on the ballot.

8) Despite the tremendous increase in the use of the initiative,
   a) relatively few actually pass.
   b) the courts have been able to make them ineffective.
   c) many of the proposed measures conflict with other provisions of law in California or the federal government.
   d) All of the above
   e) None of the above

9) Referenda
   a) are invoked as frequently as initiatives.
   b) are measures written by the voters and presented to the voters for approval.
   c) are used only in cases of amending the U.S. Constitution.
   d) allow voters to overturn laws passed by the legislature and signed by the governor.
   e) are usually easy to pass.

10) Gray Davis, reelected to serve as governor of California in 2002,
    a) was replaced by Arnold Schwarzenegger in the 2005 special election.
    b) was recalled by the voters the very next year, who also elected Arnold Schwarzenegger on the same ballot.
    c) won the right in court to add his name to the recall election ballot.
    d) believed that the recall was consistent with a republican form of government.
    e) had been caught embezzling money from the state and was therefore recalled by the people of California.

INTERNET RESOURCES

Public Policy Institute of California: **http://www.ppic.org**
State Constitution: **http://www.leginfo.ca.gov/const-toc.html**
Secretary of State's: **http://www.ss.ca.gov**
League of Women Voters: **http://www.lwv.org**
The California Voter Foundation: **http://www.calvoter.org/index.html**
Project Vote Smart: **http://www.vote-smart.org**

CHAPTER 5: *INTEREST GROUPS AND POLITICAL PARTIES IN CALIFORNIA*

INTRODUCTION

Intimately tied to voting and participation, interest groups and political parties play a role in the political lives of Californians. While the Progressives undermined the stronghold of the political parties in the early 1900s, political parties continue to play a role in state politics through the organization of the state legislature, but they have a much more subdued role in voter identification. The relative weakness of the political parties in California has created opportunities for interest groups to mobilize and in many cases supplement and even supplant the role of the party. The twenty-first century has not revived California voters' interest in the political parties, as events at the end of the twentieth century eroded party identification in the electorate; the parties are still important in the functions of the government.

While there are similarities between political parties and interest groups, their functions and accountability to the electorate differ greatly. Political parties and interest groups both serve as intermediaries between citizens and the people in government who make the decisions that affect the lives of Californians. They both bring Californians together who share common interests and amplify people's voices when speaking to government. Both raise issues for government to address and bring back information about what government is doing to their members. Some of the major distinctions, however, include the role of each in the electoral and governance process. Parties focus on nominating candidates, helping elect them, and organizing the activities of those who win. Once in office, the party serves as an organizing agent, bringing the members together to vote a particular way on an issue, and assigning members to key committees. For this reason, voters can hold the political parties accountable at election time if they decide they are not happy with the decisions of their candidates. Most organized interests represent much narrower groups, as members of interest groups typically share a much narrower agenda. Since most interest groups are interested in a handful of policy issues only, they do not have the same membership base as the parties. In addition, while interest groups may be committed to nominating and electing certain candidates to serve in California's government because they would like to elect a person who shares their beliefs on a particular policy item, interest groups are just as likely to try to influence the government once the candidate is elected through lobbying the government and educating its members.

INTEREST GROUPS

Interest groups are groups of people who organize to influence government and public policy. Californians can voice their opinions more effectively through an interest group that has been organized to promote a specific policy preference or ideology. Several features of California's government help facilitate the formation of interest groups. The first is the relative weakness of California's political parties. Political parties are the organizations through which citizens seek to govern; their goal is to win elections. While interest groups may choose to support candidates who support their policy preferences, their goals are mostly policy oriented and therefore do not have the same accountability to the public. One legacy of the progressive reforms in California is that political parties do not have the organizing and mobilization forces that they have elsewhere, leaving a vacuum for interest groups to fill.

Interest Groups in California

The framers of the United States Constitution were concerned about the effects of faction as contrary to the public good. In *Federalist 10*, James Madison warns of the dangers of faction, which could comprise either a majority or minority of the population organized for the principle of pursuing selfish interests to the detriment of the public. More recently, social scientists have observed the imbalance of power among groups of people, favoring the elite and those with money.

Interest groups play an important role in California politics, and if viewed through this light, they are important instruments in a democracy, serving the public interest. Interest groups convey public desires to government officials better than elections do because they are usually policy-specific while elections only convey voters' frustrations or approval of a policymaker. In addition, theoretically, anyone may join or organize a group that reflects his or her own interests. The frequency of elections and the initiative process invites the formation of interest groups in California; there is strength in numbers. Interest groups provide the backbone for organizing; organizing may take the form of petition signature drives, demonstrations, email and letter-writing campaigns, or even visits with legislators, executives, and bureaucrats.

The Progressives were more concerned about the connection between corporations and political parties and therefore sought to emancipate politics from the parties. The reforms they passed at the turn of the twentieth century reflect this concern. However, it is clear that as a result, interest groups have had ample opportunity to develop and hone their skills. Their role in California politics is increasingly evident as they flex their muscle in the initiative process. The Progressives sought to break the party machine so as to open the political process to the people; the direct democracy they established may have had the undesired effect of turning the process directly into the hands of special interests and corporations.

The formation of an interest group, while arguably available to anyone, is an expensive endeavor, requiring specific political knowledge and skills. Interest groups are therefore almost exclusively the product of a small, well-financed minority of people. Their functions include lobbying and campaigning for and against public policy in the form of initiative and referenda.

Interest Group Activities

Any group that perceives itself or its concerns as being affected by government may engage in these activities. The efforts interest groups may take depend on whether they are interested in preserving an existing law and resisting change or are supporting an amended version or a wholesale change. Organized letter-writing, protests, and even lawsuits all are means by which interest groups influence policymakers in the legislature and executive branches. For example, in spring 2007, the California Supreme Court heard the case *Viva! International Voice for Animals et al.* v. *Adidas Promotional Retail Operations et al.* that was brought to court by the interest group Viva! International Voice for Animals, acting with the Humane Society. The interest groups asked the California Supreme Court to reinstate a law prohibiting the importation and sale of designated wildlife products and parts. However, the court process is usually slow and unpredictable; therefore, the most obvious method to influence government policy is to hire a lobbyist.

A lobbyist is a person whose job is to influence policymakers. In some instances, major corporations or public interest groups hire their own advocates. More frequently, however, interests hire contract lobbyists who work under contract for a number of clients. Ethically, the lobbyists must be sure that the interests of their clients do not conflict, but the system works well for many. The lobbyist's job includes tracking bills as they are introduced and talking to members of the legislature and the governor's staff about their clients' position. While many clients donate money to political campaigns, and while it is certainly true that the lobbyists influence these donations and have better access to legislators to whom their clients have donated, lobbyists themselves ordinarily do not give significant campaign dollars.

A second and often more hidden function of interest groups is to promote or obstruct new laws through the initiative process. The initiative process is a good way for interest groups to influence policy since the results have the potential to add a new law or constitutional amendment to California's code. The initiative process is therefore attractive to wealthy and narrow interests who are single-mindedly in pursuit of a policy goal. In addition, California law limits the amount of money an interest group can contribute to a candidate running for office, therefore limiting the amount of influence any interest may have over a candidate; spending on initiative campaigns, however, is not restricted, and wealthy organized interests can spend freely to influence the voters. Another attractive feature of the initiative process is that it allows interest groups to paint a picture for the voters to sway their opinions. Voters tend to rely on party cues and name recognition in voting for candidates, but often these are absent in the initiative campaign. In addition, the subject matter of many of the initiatives may be very complex and voters may not have all the information and resources to make an informed decision. This forces the voters to rely on the information provided by the interest group that is proposing the legislation in the first place—not a particularly objective review of information. Finally, it may be unclear which interest group is sponsoring a particular initiative, and voters will not have full information as to the sponsors; this may benefit some of the less popular interest groups or those who would clearly have a vested interest economically in the outcome.

Research indicates that economic interest groups that can raise and mobilize monetary resources spend the majority of their resources to defeat ballot measures and preserve the status quo. Conversely, citizen interest groups mobilize personnel resources and spend money to support initiatives.[40] In a 1998 study, economic interests spent nearly $99 million to oppose initiatives, while citizen groups spent only $33 million.[41] However, the impact of the spending is less clear: initiatives supported by citizen interests had higher passage rates than those supported by economic interests. Nevertheless, the fears of the framers and Progressives and the observations of social scientists were well founded.

Regulation of Interest Groups in California

Historically, California's lobbyists have been extremely powerful. During and immediately after the Depression, Artie Samish was the dominant lobbyist. Samish represented breweries, racetracks, railroads, and other major industries. He eventually claimed publicly that he controlled the legislature through his monetary donations. In response, the legislature passed the first regulations of lobbyists. The Collier Act required that lobbyists disclose their employers and report the total amount, divided into general categories that they spent on lobbying.

Much more restrictive reform arrived in 1974 in the form of the Political Reform Act. As is typical of California, this sweeping legislation was an initiative. The sponsors were then-Democratic Secretary of State Jerry Brown, Common Cause, and the People's Lobby. Under the PRA, all lobbyists were required to register and file detailed reports of income and spending with the secretary of state's office and the Fair Political Practices Commission (FPPC). The FPPC was created by the initiative as a watchdog over both lobbyists and candidates. The PRA also limited lobbyists to expenditures of $10 per month per public official. Prior to this, it was common practice for lobbyists to "wine and dine" legislators and staff as means of creating access to them.

California's secretary of state's office keeps track of the activities of lobbyists and lobbying firms. The office maintains a database of all registered lobbyists in California, including individuals, firms, and lobbyist employers. Moreover, the secretary of state's office tracks lobbying-related activities as well. This information can be found online at http://cal-access.ss.ca.gov/Lobbying.

California Interest Groups. There are 12 main categories of interest groups in California and they include: Agriculture; Business and Economy; Education; Energy; Environment; Health; Labor; Law Enforcement; Legal; Public Interest and Political Reform; Recreation and Transportation; and Social Issues. Social issues represent a broad array of interests, including the following groups: California Housing Law Project; California Peace Action; Christian Coalition of California; Death Penalty Focus of California; Log Cabin Republicans of Orange County; National Rifle Association of California; Protection and Advocacy Inc. (advancing the human and legal rights of people with disabilities); Center for the Advancement of Nonviolence.[42]

---

[40] Gerber, Elisabeth, 1998. *Interest Group Influence in the California Initiative Process*, Public Policy Institute of California.
[41] Gerber, 1998.
[42] The California Voter Foundation, August 22, 2005.

THE PARTIES

Prior to the progressive reforms, California was effectively ruled by major landholders, particularly the railroads. The tool through which they governed was the Republican Party. Republicans were the clear majority in the state; the party's nominees were selected at conventions, and the railroad barons controlled the conventions. Thus, when the Progressives sought to devolve power to the people, their first target was the political party. They instituted the direct primary to replace nominating conventions, enabling all registered members of a party to have input into its nominations. They then passed laws prohibiting parties or their officials from either endorsing or giving money to candidates in these primaries. They deprived the parties of a base by making all local elections nonpartisan. They instituted a system called cross-filing, under which candidates could run in the primaries of as many parties as they wished. Under this system, members of one party sometimes won the nomination of another party. For example, Republican Earl Warren, who later became governor of California and then chief justice of the U.S. Supreme Court, was nominated for attorney general in 1938 by both the Republicans and Democrats, thus assuring his election in November. The result of these reforms was a system of very weak parties that had a difficult time even influencing who their nominees would be.

Cross-filing was abolished in 1959. A federal court decision in the 1980s removed the limits on party endorsements and donations, but by then the pattern was firmly established. Republicans still prohibit the practice by their own rules while the Democrats allow it but have rarely exercised it. California's experiment with different modes of primary elections has also likely weakened the voters' commitment to parties. Even before Californians passed the blanket primary, voters were declining to state a partisan affiliation when they registered, apparently unhappy with both the major parties. The blanket primary, which was used in 1998 and 2000, made participating without a party affiliation even easier. Despite the United States Supreme Court's ruling in 2000 that the blanket primary violated the parties' rights to association and demand that California amend its primary system, the modified closed primary continues to offer registered voters who have declined to state a party affiliation an opportunity to participate in a primary election. Those who have declined to state an affiliation with a political party must request the ballot of a political party if authorized by the party's rules and duly noted by the Secretary of State if they want to participate in the party's primary election; otherwise, they are provided a nonpartisan ballot, containing only the names of candidates for nonpartisan offices and measures to be voted upon at the primary election.

Overall, however, the modified closed primaries, the ability of parties to endorse candidates in primaries and nonpartisan races, and the utilization of parties as conduits for campaign contributions under Proposition 34 have made the parties stronger than the Progressives intended them to be. But they remain weaker than those in many other states, especially in the East.

Major Parties

In California, as in the rest of the country, two parties can hope to win a majority of the votes: Republicans and Democrats. People who have a conservative ideology believe most day-to-day operations are better left to local control and market forces, align with the Republican Party. The Republican Party tends to address issues of concern to business and law and order. People who are more liberal and believe that the government should address the needs of the people of California through public programs and public assistance align best with the Democratic Party. The Democratic Party tends to address issues regarding civil rights for minorities, public assistance for low-income households, and health care. A majority of registered Democrats in the state are women while a majority of Republicans are men. According to the secretary of state's office, in September 2010 there were 23,521,995 eligible voters and 16,993,075 registered voters in California. Of these, 44.3 percent were Democrats and 30.9 percent were Republicans; members of third parties account for 4.6 percent of the California electorate. The remaining portion of registered voters "decline to state," comprising 20.2 percent of registered voters, and the fastest-growing category. Table 5:1 below shows the top 10 counties in terms of party registration.

Table 5:1 – Political Party Registration by County

Democratic Party		Republican Party		Decline to State	
Alameda	57.32%	Modoc	48.96%	San Francisco	29.54%
San Francisco	56.48%	Placer	48.39%	Santa Clara	26.66%
Santa Cruz	54.95%	Lassen	47.91%	Mono	24.74%
Marin	54.70%	Shasta	47.34%	San Mateo	23.59%
Monterey	53.39%	Sutter	46.35%	San Diego	23.06%
Sonoma	52.24%	Colusa	46.00%	Alpine	22.34%
San Mateo	52.01%	Madera	45.70%	Alameda	22.33%
Imperial	51.98%	Glenn	45.69%	Yolo	21.92%
Los Angeles	51.63%	Tulare	45.59%	Humboldt	21.80%
Contra Costa	50.15%	Amador	45.35%	Marin	21.66%

Source: California Secretary of State Web site, September 2010

Historically more Californians have registered as Democrats although registered Democrats and Republicans have been decreasing; in 2010 the percentage of Democrats remained roughly equal to the percentage in 2008 . Nonetheless, "Decline to State" voters have been increasing rapidly. In 2010, over 20 percent of registered California voters declined to state a party affiliation. Figure 5:1 illustrates this history.

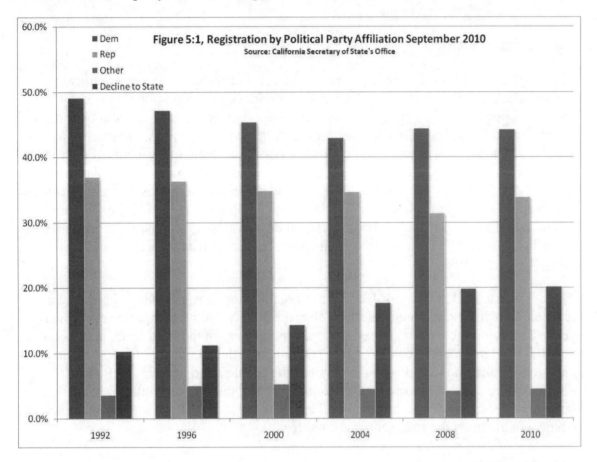

Figure 5:1, Registration by Political Party Affiliation September 2010
Source: California Secretary of State's Office

Minor Parties

While the two major parties receive the bulk of the money and media attention, and consequently win virtually all the partisan seats, there are five minor parties in the state. It is not impossible for these third parties to qualify for the ballot. A new third party must either register at least 1 percent of California's voters into the party or persuade 10 percent of the voters to sign a petition asking that the party be placed on the ballot. Even a non-qualified party can get its presidential and vice presidential candidates on the ballot if it can persuade 1 percent of the voters to sign a petition. This latter category of candidate is listed as "independent."

The five third parties are Libertarian, American Independent, Green, Reform, and Natural Law. Like all minor parties, their role generally is to highlight issues that the major parties avoid and to serve as an alternative for voters who are frustrated with the Republicans and Democrats. "Other" in Figure 5:1 illustrates third party membership in the state of California.

While the major parties dominate state-elected posts, occasionally a third party will succeed in electing one of their candidates. In a special election on March 30, 1999, Audie Bock from Alameda County was elected to the legislature as a Green Party candidate. Although she later changed her party affiliation to Independent, her victory sent a message to the two major parties that she represented a group of voters who were disenchanted with the major parties.

Party Organization

The Progressives also dictated the structures that still characterize today's political parties. The governing body of each party is the state central committee. This body is composed primarily of the party's partisan elected officials and unsuccessful nominees for partisan office, plus individuals appointed by those two groups. Various other people are also included, such as past party chairmen, county chairmen, presidents of auxiliaries recognized by the party, etc. The central committees adopt the party's state platform, raise money for party candidates in the general election, and adopt resolutions reflecting the positions of the party. The Democratic central committee, known as the California Democratic Party (CDP), may also endorse candidates in statewide partisan primaries by a two-thirds vote. The Republican central committee, known as the California Republican Party (CRP), has rules that forbid such a practice.

There is also a legal but very different party organization in each county. The party's registered voters in the primary election elect the county central committee every two years. The committees are supposed to organize the party at the local level, get out the vote (GOTV) in general elections, adopt resolutions reflecting the opinions of the local party, and replace nominees who die between the primary and general elections. Following Progressive precepts for weakening parties, there is very little coordination between the state party and the county parties. The most direct link is the membership of county chairmen on the state central committee.

Funding Elections

Unlike the federal government, California has imposed few restrictions on campaign funding. Individuals and groups have been able to give unlimited amounts, and campaigns have been able to spend unlimited amounts. Most of the money has been provided by political action committees (PACs), organizations through which interest groups direct dollars to favored candidates or campaigns.

Interest groups find the initiative process a much easier way to spend money. The U.S. Supreme Court has ruled that legislation cannot limit spending on initiatives because an initiative campaign is unlike a candidate campaign, and there is no risk of corruption in the initiative campaign. However, contributions to congressional campaigns and campaigns for the state legislature are limited by law. So groups find the initiative process an attractive way to influence legislation, spending as much as they can.

During the 1974 primary election, voters overwhelmingly approved the Political Reform Act, establishing the Fair Political Practices Commission (FPPC) to administer and enforce its provisions. Candidates and campaigns (such as initiative campaigns) must report how much money they receive and where they spend it. Every donation of $100 or more must be identified by its source. Donations in cash of $100 or more are illegal. PACs must register with the secretary of state, and their donations must be reported with their state identification numbers. Individual donors must be identified by name, address, and occupation. The FPPC enforces these laws and fines violators.

In 2000, Californians passed the latest of a series of proposals intended to limit the role of money in campaigns. Proposition 34, which took effect for the legislature in 2002, caps single donations to legislative candidates at $3,300, and to gubernatorial candidates at $22,300. Political parties, however, are exempt from these restrictions as well as from local limits. This provides a significant opening for abuse since groups and individuals are now encouraged to "launder" their donations through the parties.

Parties serve as points of contact between the public and its government. In California, the legislature is organized by majority and minority party, determined by which of the parties holds the greatest number of seats. The majority party elects the speaker of the assembly and the senate pro tem and controls the committees by selection of committee chairs as well as runs floor debate. Therefore, while the cohesiveness of the parties in the electorate may be uncertain, the legislature and its relationship with the executive branch is very much guided by party affiliation.

SOMETHING TO THINK ABOUT

1. What advantages do interest groups provide to the political system? What are the costs?

2. What kinds of activities do interest groups engage in to influence policy?

3. Why have the numbers of Californians who refuse to state a party in registering to vote increased?

4. How powerful are California's political parties? How do they compare with other states' party organizations?

5. Are there possibilities for third parties in California? How have third parties influenced California politics and policy?

MULTIPLE-CHOICE QUESTIONS

1) Interest groups have gained power in California because
   a) the reformers sought to increase the power of interest groups over the political parties.
   b) of the relative weakness of the political parties in the electorate.
   c) of the opportunity to influence candidates through campaign contributions.
   d) voting for state officers is nonpartisan.
   e) interest groups must follow strict rules for behavior, making them very organized.

2) Which of the following is true about BOTH political parties and interest groups?
   a) They organize the structure of the legislature.
   b) They can be held accountable in elections.
   c) They are interested in seeing certain candidates elected.
   d) They are interested in just a few policy issues.
   e) All of the above

3) In a democracy, interest groups do all of the following EXCEPT
   a) serve the public interest.
   b) convey the wishes of the public to government on specific policy goals.
   c) help Californians organize to become more politically active.
   d) allow anyone to join.
   e) serve only those with money.

4) Interest groups participate in government through
   a) litigation.
   b) lobbying.
   c) organizing for demonstrations.
   d) funding initiatives.
   e) All of the above

5) The initiative process is popular with interest groups because
   a) interest groups are prohibited by law from speaking with lawmakers about their policy preferences, and the initiative process allows them to make policy and bypass the legislature.
   b) interest groups typically do not have the kind of resources necessary to contribute to candidates to influence the eventual lawmaker.
   c) it helps them to attract new members because their names will be frequently cited in commercials and advertisements.
   d) there are limits to the amounts interest groups may contribute to candidate campaigns but not to initiative campaigns.
   e) they do not cost the interest group very much because voters are typically familiar with the issues being raised.

6) A major reform of the Progressives to divest control away from the parties was
   a) the blanket primary.
   b) party conventions.
   c) the direct primary.
   d) direct endorsement of candidates during the nomination.
   e) the modified closed primary.

7) More voters in California are currently registered as
   a) "decline to state."
   b) Republicans.
   c) Democrats.
   d) independents.
   e) third-party members.

8) The dramatic increase in the number of voters who have declined to state a party affiliation is the result of
   a) the costs of joining a party.
   b) the amount of knowledge required to vote along party lines.
   c) dissatisfaction with the two dominant parties.
   d) the relative ease with which the change in primary laws allows nonidentified partisans to participate.
   e) C and D only

9) Despite the concerns of the Progressives with regard to interest groups and their efforts to wrest control from them with direct democracy,
   a) they had nothing to fear because interest groups are well regulated and do not hold power in the state.
   b) interest groups have used the initiative process to their advantage, bypassing the legislature to make law, and influencing the voters.
   c) interest groups are usually not successful in the initiative process.
   d) interest groups generally rely on lobbyists for influence.
   e) interest groups influence the political parties to get what they want.

10) The principal organizing structure of the political parties in California is
   a) the state central committee.
   b) GOTV.
   c) PAC.
   d) the county central committee.
   e) the local organizing committee.

INTERNET RESOURCES

State Constitution: **http://www.leginfo.ca.gov/const-toc.html**
Secretary of State: **http://www.ss.ca.gov**
The California Voter Foundation: **http://www.calvoter.org/index.html**
Project Vote Smart: **http://www.vote-smart.org**
California Democratic Party: **http://www.ca-dem.org**
California Republican Party: **http://cagop.org**
Counting California: **http://countingcalifornia.cdlib.org**

CHAPTER 6: *THE LEGISLATIVE BRANCH*

INTRODUCTION

Article IV of California's constitution establishes the legislature as the lawmaking branch of California's government. Reasserting California's commitment to direct democracy, Section 1 of the article reads, "The legislative power of this State is vested in the California Legislature which consists of the senate and assembly, but the people reserve to themselves the powers of initiative and referendum."[43]

Like all states except Nebraska, California has a bicameral (two-house) legislature. In order to serve in the California Legislature, members must be over 18 years old, and citizens of the United States and of California. Article IV, Section 2(c) establishes a residency requirement, which mandates that the member be a resident of the legislative district for one year, and a citizen of the United States and a resident of California for three years immediately preceding the election.[44] These provisions conflict with federal court decisions and are therefore unenforceable.[45]

CALIFORNIA'S PROFESSIONAL LEGISLATURE

California has the nation's most professionalized legislature in terms of the compensation, staff, office expense budgets, and legislative demands.[46] As we might expect in progressive California, the people have had a direct voice in creating many of the rules governing the legislature. In 1966, under the compulsory referendum, they created a full-time legislature. In 1990, the voters passed Proposition 112, establishing the Citizens Compensation Commission, which sets legislative salaries. The reform spirit was strident in 1990, and several initiatives were passed that year, setting limits on terms, salaries, benefits, and office staff.

Legislative Sessions

In 1972 Californians adopted Proposition 4, which created two-year legislative sessions. The session begins on the first Monday in December of even-numbered years and must adjourn by midnight November 30 of the following even-numbered year. The constitution provides that the governor may call the legislature into special session by proclamation.[47] During these "extraordinary" sessions, the legislature must consider those subjects specified in the governor's proclamation. Proposition 140, passed in 1990, created a number of reforms, including legislative term limits. Today, members of the assembly may serve no more than three two-year terms in that chamber. Senators are limited to two four-year terms. The result is an influx of new members who have very limited experience.

---

[43] Section 1, Article IV, California Constitution.
[44] Section 2 (c), Article IV California Constitution.
[45] "Legislators' Districts, Qualifications, Terms, and Compensation," California's Legislature http://www.leginfo.ca.gov/pdf/caleg7.pdf, p. 85.
[46] Maestas, Cherie, 2003. The Incentive to Listen: Progressive Ambition, Resources, and Opinion Monitoring among State Legislators, *The Journal of Politics* Vol 65:2.
[47] Article IV, Section 3(b) California Constitution.

Compensation and Resources

The California Citizens Compensation Commission sets the salaries for members of the state legislature. The commission voted to increase the salaries of legislators in December 2006. Current annual salary for members of both houses is $113,098, plus a tax-free *per diem* allowance of $125 for every day they are on official state business. In addition, members receive a monthly allowance to lease a car, a gasoline credit card, and a telephone credit card. The speaker of the assembly and the senate pro tem earn even more, currently $130,062 annually. Proposition 140, passed in 1990, cut legislative staff by 25 percent, abolished the legislative pension plan, and created term limits.

Structure of the Legislature

As discussed above, California's legislature is bicameral; the lower chamber of the legislature is the assembly, and the upper chamber is the senate.

Caucuses

A caucus is an informal group of legislators who are identified by a common identity, policy position, or goal. They do not have a formal role in the legislative process the way committees do, but they have significant influence over their respective members and the types of policy discussed in the legislature. The assembly currently has 10 different caucuses. There are many assembly members who are members of more than one caucus. The current legislative caucuses include: Democratic Caucus; Republican Caucus; Asian Pacific Islander Caucus; Black Caucus; Latino Caucus; LGBT Caucus; Rural Caucus; Smart Growth Caucus; Legislative Women's Caucus. There are eight caucuses in the senate, including: Senate Democratic Caucus; Senate Republican Caucus; Latino Legislative Caucus; Legislative Black Caucus; Legislative Internet Caucus; Legislative LGBT Caucus; Legislative Rural Caucus; Legislative Women's Caucus.

California Assembly

Membership. The assembly has 80 members who serve two-year terms. Each assembly member represents roughly 440,000 constituents. Any member elected after November 1990 is restricted to three terms for a total of six years in the state assembly. If a candidate is elected to fill more than half the remaining term of a previously elected member, the entire term will be counted toward the candidate's total number of terms.

Representation. Assembly districts are based on population. Every 10 years, according to the federal census, district lines are reconsidered. The map below details the 80 California Assembly districts.[48] After the November 2008 elections, the Assembly will host 50 Democrats and 30 Republicans; Democrats gained two seats in the Assembly but needed six to reach the two-thirds majority required to pass a state spending plan.

---

[48] From the California State Legislature Web site.

Specific Powers and Duties. Unlike the United States House of Representatives, there are fewer specific powers in California's lower chamber. The assembly has the sole power of impeachment. Impeachment extends to officers elected on a statewide basis, members of the State Board of Equalization, and judges of state courts for misconduct in office.[49]

California Senate

Membership. The senate has 40 members who serve four-year terms. Each senator represents roughly 846,791 Californians.[50] As a result of Proposition 140, passed in 1990, members elected after November 1990 are restricted to two terms, for a total of eight years in the state senate. One half of the senate membership is elected every two years. The map below details the 40 California Senate districts.[51]

Specific Powers and Duties. The California Senate has few powers unique to the chamber. Impeachments are tried by the senate and conviction requires a two-thirds vote. The senate's judgment may extend only to removal from office and disqualification to hold any office under the state.

---

[49] Article IV, Section 18.
[50] California Senate Web site, http://www.senate.ca.gov/.
[51] From the California State Legislature Web site.

PRESIDING OFFICERS

Assembly: The Dominant Speaker

The presiding officer in the California Assembly is the speaker. The California Constitution stipulates that at the beginning of the legislative term, the assembly must elect a speaker. He or she presides over the chamber, directs debate, appoints other leadership positions from within the assembly, and assigns bills to committees. The speaker appoints a speaker pro tempore and an assistant speaker pro tempore, whose duties are to preside over the sessions of the assembly in the event of the absence of the speaker. Given that the speaker represents the majority party, he or she will appoint a majority floor leader and the Minority Party Caucus appoints a minority floor leader. The real power of the assembly speaker, however, lies in his or her ability to appoint and remove the members and chairs of all standing committees except Rules. He or she also assigns offices to members. All this gives the speaker tremendous control over the political lives of the assembly members, especially since their abilities to influence legislation and raise campaign dollars are heavily influenced by their committee assignments. Furthermore, since the speaker has such control over the committees, he or she has significant control of legislation, and, therefore, overwhelming fundraising abilities. Modern speakers spread these campaign dollars among their party's members and candidates, further increasing their influence. In addition, in the assembly, the members will elect a person who is not a member of the legislature to serve as chief clerk, sergeant at arms, and chaplain by a majority vote.

Legendary speakers have left lasting marks on California's political landscape. Jesse Unruh (D-Inglewood) was responsible for the successful campaign for Proposition 1A, which created a nationally envied, full-time professional legislature. Willie Brown (D-San Francisco) was the longest serving Speaker (1980 to 1995) and the self-proclaimed "ayatollah of the assembly." Unruh, after losing the governorship to Ronald Reagan in 1970, was elected Treasurer four years later and greatly enhanced the power and prestige of that office. Brown was forced from the assembly by term limits but was elected Mayor of San Francisco in 1996 and served through 2004.

Normally, the speaker is a member of the majority party in the Assembly. The Majority Caucus (a meeting of all the members of the majority party in the assembly) makes its choice. A vote on the floor follows, but since one candidate is supported by the majority, he or she usually wins. There have been exceptions. In 1980, the majority Democrats split, and Willie Brown was elected Speaker by a coalition of some Democrats and eight Republicans. In 1994, following complicated maneuvers in an almost evenly divided chamber, Republican Doris Allen became speaker with the votes of all the Democrats as well as her own. When enraged Republicans removed her from office in a recall, Republican Brian Setencich briefly became speaker in the same manner.

The current speaker is John A. Perez, (D-46) who assumed the Speakership after Karen Bass. Bass became speaker in May 2008 and made history as the sixty-seventh speaker of the California State Assembly, the first Democratic woman in the speakership, and the first African American woman in the country to serve as speaker of a state house.[52]

Senate: A More Collegial Leadership

In the California Senate, no single individual possesses powers equal to those of the speaker. The president of the senate is the lieutenant governor, but he or she rarely presides and may vote only in case of a tie. The real leader is the president pro tempore, better known as the pro tem. Like the speaker, he or she is normally elected by the majority party. The pro tem chairs the Rules Committee, which controls all other committee and committee chair assignments, as well as the flow of legislation. Since Rules consists of two Democrats, two Republicans, and the pro tem, and since the pro tem is the acknowledged leader of the majority party, he or she in fact is in position to dominate the action of the chamber.

Senator Darell Steinberg, the current pro tem, is a Democrat from Sacramento. He was first elected to the Senate in 2006. He served in the Assembly from 1994-2006..

COMMITTEES

The legislature will consider about 7,000 bills in addition to numerous constitutional amendments and other resolutions during a legislative session. To help make the legislative process more manageable given the magnitude of bills proposed and the variety of the subject matter, the California Legislature has developed a system of policy committees. The work of the legislature occurs in committee. The standing committees

---

[52] Karen Bass Bio, http://democrats.assembly.ca.gov/speaker/About_Karen/Meet_Karen/default.aspx

are permanent committees that meet on a regular basis throughout the year. Citizens can raise concerns regarding proposed legislation during committee hearings. There are currently 29 standing committees in the assembly and 25 standing committees in the senate, ranging in policy domains from agriculture to transportation and public safety. Many standing committees have sub-committees that focus in more depth on particular issues. There are two additional types of committees: select committees and special committees, which study California policy issues and problems in order to develop more long-range solutions. Joint committees have membership from both houses and consider issues of joint concern.

THE LEGISLATIVE ANALYST

The Legislative Analyst's Office (LAO) is a nonpartisan office created to provide the legislature with budgetary and fiscal information. The head of the LAO is the legislative analyst, who is appointed by the Joint Legislative Budget Committee. This committee also oversees the work of the LAO.

STAFF

California has a full-time, professional legislature that includes a large staff. Each member has an individual staff, with members of the majority in each house enjoying a significant numerical advantage. Each committee is assigned staff consultants, most of who are under the control of the chair and the majority. The caucuses themselves, Democrats and Republicans, hire staff. Finally, the legislature as a whole is served by several neutral support agencies. The legislative analyst and staff are the fiscal experts, particularly in reviewing and analyzing the governor's budget. The office of the legislative counsel consists of lawyers who help draft legislation and offer legal opinions on a wide range of issues.

The state auditor reviews the financial and operational performances of agencies administering state programs. The Bureau of State Audits was created in 1993 to replace the Auditor General's Office, which closed due to budget reductions in December 1992. While the Auditor General's Office had been part of the legislative branch, the new Bureau of State Audits is part of the executive branch. To assure its independence, the state auditor is appointed by the executive but reports to the legislature, and his or her administrative operations are overseen by a state commission.

LEGISLATIVE PROPOSALS

There are several types of legislative proposals, each of which has its own purpose. These include bills and resolutions and are discussed in more detail below.

Bills

In California, all laws are enacted by the passage of bills. The word "bills" encompasses concurrent and joint resolutions and constitutional amendments as well. A bill either proposes a new law or amends or repeals the existing law. Unlike the federal Constitution, which mandates that bills raising revenue originate in the lower house, in

California the budget bill is introduced simultaneously in both houses. Bills are designated as AB for assembly bills and SB for senate bills.

There is a maximum number of bills that either a senator or assembly member may introduce in any given legislative session. Senators may introduce a total of 65 bills, while the assembly member may introduce 30 bills. There are additional rules imposed on bill introduction, including the Joint Rule deadline for bill introduction, which stipulates that only committee bills, constitutional amendments, assembly bills approved by the speaker, and senate bills approved by the Senate Committee on Rules may be introduced.[53]

Resolutions

There are four kinds of resolutions used in the legislature. They include constitutional amendments, concurrent resolutions, joint resolutions, and house and senate resolutions. Constitutional amendments are a unique kind of resolution, requiring a two-thirds approval by both legislative chambers while the remaining three require a majority vote for passage. Concurrent resolutions and joint resolutions require consideration and adoption by both houses of the legislature before they can take effect. House (assembly) and senate resolutions are only considered within their respective chambers.

Constitutional Amendments. Legislative constitutional amendments are resolutions that propose amendments to the state constitution. The legislature may propose constitutional amendments and require two-thirds of the members of each house to support the proposal. Following the legislature's approval, the amendment must be submitted to California voters directly. A constitutional amendment may only be adopted and ratified by a majority vote of the qualified voters before it becomes a part of California's constitution. Constitutional amendments are identified as ACA, which stands for Assembly Constitutional Amendment, or SCA, Senate Constitutional Amendment.

Joint Resolutions. The California Legislature dedicates joint resolutions to those matters associated with the federal government. Joint resolutions are distinguished from other types of legislation by the initials AJR, for Assembly Joint Resolution, or SJR, for Senate Joint Resolution. Joint resolutions express the approval or disapproval of members of California's legislature of pending or proposed congressional legislation or programs and activities of the federal government. California also uses joint resolutions to ratify amendments to the United States Constitution.

Concurrent Resolutions. Concurrent resolutions are used for measures that must be addressed by both houses of the legislature but handle internal legislative matters only. Concurrent resolutions are indicated by ACR (Assembly Concurrent Resolution) or SCR (Senate Concurrent Resolution). The legislature uses concurrent resolutions, which require a majority vote from both houses, for a variety of purposes, including the adoption of Joint Rules, creating joint committees, directing executive departments to

---

[53] The Legislative Process, The Legislature, http://www.leginfo.ca.gov/califleg.html.

make specific reports to the legislature, and memorializing the death of a member or a former member of the legislature or their immediate families.[54]

House and Senate Resolutions. Each chamber may pass resolutions affecting its internal operations and procedures through a single house resolution. They are expressions of just one house of the legislature. A single house resolution in the assembly is designated HR (House Resolution) and SR (Senate Resolution) in the senate. These resolutions are used to amend the house rules, to create committees, or to request a committee of the house to study a specific problem.

LEGISLATIVE PROCESS

The procedure for passing a bill into law in California involves a complex system of committees and rules and requires the signature of the governor or a veto override by the legislature. The idea for a proposed law may come from many sources: legislators and their staffs, the governor, governmental agencies, interest groups, even private citizens. A legislator in the chamber of which he or she is a member, however, must introduce the proposal itself.

Bill Introduction

A legislator acts as the sponsor of the bill, authors the measure, and sends the idea and language for the bill to the Legislative Counsel. The formal bill, which is drafted by the Legislative Counsel, is returned to the legislator for introduction and given a number at the first reading. The first reading requires that the clerk read the bill number, the name of the author, and the descriptive title of the bill. The bill is then sent electronically to the Office of State Printing. A bill must be in print for 30 days to allow for public review before it continues in the legislative process. The bill then goes to the Senate or Assembly Rules Committee, where it is assigned to the appropriate policy committee for its first hearing.

Committee Referral and Consideration

Bills are assigned to committees according to their subject area. Most bills live or die at this stage. Committees conduct hearings to gather information regarding the policy and its possible consequences. During the hearing the author presents the bill, and people and various interest groups testify in support or opposition of the bill. The committee can pass the bill by a majority vote of the membership of the committee, amend the bill and pass the bill as amended, or defeat the bill. Bills that require money must also be heard in the Fiscal Committee, and the senate and assembly appropriations committees. If a committee, after holding hearings, votes not to recommend a bill, it dies for that session. If the committee recommends "Do Pass" with a unanimous or nearly unanimous vote, then colleagues are more likely to support that bill when it comes up for debate. At the second reading, bills that have passed out of committee are read again on the floor and scheduled for debate.

---

[54] The Legislative Process, The Legislature, http://www.leginfo.ca.gov/califleg.html.

Floor debate takes place during a third reading, where bills are passed or defeated by the entire chamber on a roll call vote. During the third reading, the bill is explained by the author or a designee, discussed by the members, and voted on by a roll call vote. Most bills need only a positive vote by a majority of all members to pass, which is 21 in the senate and 41 in the assembly. Any emergency bill, or any bill that spends or taxes, however, must receive a two-thirds positive vote, 27 and 57 members respectively. The state budget in particular needs a two-thirds vote, which gives the minority party increased influence.

If a bill successfully passes one chamber, it moves on to the second chamber, where the same process occurs. If the second house passes the bill, but with amendments (changes), it is returned to the first chamber to see if they concur (agree). If they do not, the bill is assigned to a conference committee, made up of members of both the assembly and senate, to work out the differences. If they cannot agree, the bill dies. If they do agree, both chambers must vote to support the compromise.

Action by the Governor

If both chambers are agreed on the language of the bill, the bill is sent to the governor for action. The governor, after receiving a bill from the senate or assembly, has 12 days in which to sign or veto it. Should the governor fail to take any action, the bill becomes law without a signature. If the governor vetoes it, the bill is returned with a list of objections, to the house of origin. The veto may be overridden by a two-thirds majority of both houses. The legislature has 60 calendar days to act after receiving the veto. If the members are not able to gather two-thirds support for the override or have not taken any action, the veto is effective.

THE BUDGET

Passing the budget in California has become an increasingly cumbersome task involving complex interactions with the governor. The governor submits a budget to each house comprised of a complete plan and itemized statement of all proposed expenditures of the state, including both existing programs as governed by existing law and recommendations for future and existing programs. The budget proposal contains all estimated revenues for the ensuing fiscal year. The governor's budget proposal should explain the spending for the preceding fiscal year and an estimate of project expenditures. An appropriation bill, called the budget bill, is drafted reflecting the governor's proposed budget, introduced in each house of the legislature, and referred to the Assembly Budget Committee and the Senate Budget and Fiscal Review Committee, respectively. Appropriations of money from the General Fund must be passed by a two-thirds roll call vote of the membership of each house, a measure instituted by initiative. The only exception is appropriations for public school purposes. This number has posed immense hurdles for the legislature, granting enormous power to the minority party since they need only one-third plus one to prevent the budget from passing.

While the California Constitution requires that the legislature pass the budget bill by midnight, June 15, the budget bill has failed to gather sufficient support for a timely passage in several years. To fill in the gaps, the legislature has to pass emergency gap legislation to keep the government running. The budget agreement in 2010 was no different. The state is facing with large budget deficits and still reeling from economic woes, California's legislators began to approve a $126 billion state budget, 99 days late. This beat the previous record of passage, September 23, 85 days late in 2008 making it a deadline-breaking record. The budget includes a $3.5 billion dollar cut to the public school system, already under fiscal attack..

The governor has the constitutional authority to eliminate items through his item veto. These eliminated items from the budget bill are reconsidered separately and the item veto may be overridden in the same manner as bills. The governor may approve or veto one or more items of appropriation in a bill containing several items of appropriation. The governor, however, may not change a proposed law by striking out parts of a bill. Governor Schwarzenegger has promised to use his line-item veto authority to make further cuts, so although the legislature agreed on $126 billion for the budget, it is likely to be decreased; last year's budget was $119 billion.

REAPPORTIONMENT

Every 10 years, the federal government conducts a census, which is a count of the population of the United States. Since all congressional and state legislative districts must contain equal numbers of residents, the lines of districts for the House of Representatives, state senate, and assembly must be redrawn after the census to account for population shifts. The location of these lines is of paramount importance to the legislators since they determine what sorts of people will be voting for them and, therefore, their chances of winning.

Historically the actual drawing of the lines is done by the legislature through the passage of three bills, one for each body. The governor signs or vetoes these bills, just as he or she does any other law. These laws are subject to the optional referendum. If one party controls majorities in both the assembly and senate as well as the governorship, it will try to draw lines to favor its candidates at the expense of the other party. This is called gerrymandering. California has a history of partisan gerrymandering of districts to protect incumbents. This makes it harder for one party to take a seat from another.

The most recent census was conducted in 2000, and the new lines were drawn in 2001. Since the Democrats held majorities in both houses of the legislature, and since Gray Davis, a Democrat, was the governor, the new districts continue to favor Democratic incumbents and candidates. However, fearing federal legal challenges from a Republican administration, most Republican districts remained safe as well. The resulting districts offered very few competitive races between the two major parties. As a result, as part of a larger package of initiatives, Republican governor Schwarzenegger proposed Proposition 77 in the 2005 special election, which would have changed the constitution's redistricting rules; it failed in the special election. However, Edward "Ted" Costa proposed a new constitutional amendment through the initiative, Proposition 11, a legislative redistricting measure, which passed in the November 2008 elections. The law wrests control away from the Democrat-controlled Legislature and gives it to a citizens' commission.[55] The story is not over however, as the 2010 midterm elections presented voters another opportunity to decide how district lines might be drawn with two propositions. Proposition 20, winning with 61% of the vote is a constitutional amendment amending 2008's Prop 11 by removing elected representatives from the process of redrawing congressional districts and transferring the authority to the commission established in November 2008. Proposition 27 was an initiatives to repeal Proposition 11 and return the authority to draw district lines to the elected representatives, which failed with only 41% support.

TERM LIMITS

Term limits have not necessarily had the expected result in the California Legislature that its proponents sought. The claim was that it would bring more minorities and women into the fold. While there is some evidence this has happened, the inclusion has been much slower as women who are term limited from their seats are replaced by men in some cases. We have also seen more minority candidates begin to run, something to track in the coming years. Some shifts, however, do appear to have taken place on the Sacramento scene. The most obvious is the increased power of the governor, interest groups, and the senate. Despite the overwhelming power of the assembly speaker, term limits have precluded the acquisition of power reminiscent of predecessors such as Jesse Unruh or Willie Brown. Pro terms, on the other hand, tend to be people who have already served in the lower chamber and therefore understand the ways of Sacramento far better than the speakers. In addition, scholars have noted less collegiality and an increased reliance on staff and bureaucracy.

SOMETHING TO THINK ABOUT

1. How does California's professional legislature differ from the part-time legislatures in other states?

2. How have term limits impacted Californians and their lawmakers?

3. How have term limits increased opportunities for special interest groups?

4. How has the initiative process impacted the work of the legislative branches? How has it impacted the relationship between the governor and the legislature?

5. Given the impact that laws have on our daily lives, why are Californians not more concerned about the activities of the legislature? What problems does this present?

---

[55] McGreevy, Patrick 2008. "Democrats fall short of their goal of a super majority" November 6, 2008 *Los Angeles Times*

MULTIPLE-CHOICE QUESTIONS

1) All of the following are true about California's legislature EXCEPT
   a) it has two chambers—an assembly and a senate.
   b) the senate is the lower chamber.
   c) in order to serve in the California legislature, members must be over 18 years old, and citizens of the United States and of California.
   d) the legislature shares legislative power with the people.
   e) California's constitution contains a residency requirement, although it conflicts with federal law.

2) California's legislature has been shaped by
   a) direct democracy, which has made it the least professionalized in the country.
   b) a statute passed by the legislature that created a Citizens Compensation Commission.
   c) the Progressive spirit that was evident in the 1990s, which was fearful of the accumulation of power but also a lack of accountability.
   d) direct democracy, which gave control to the governor to call regular legislative sessions.
   e) governor control over the number of terms assembly members and state senators may serve.

3) The California Assembly
   a) has 40 members.
   b) has a limit of six terms total.
   c) is based on population, which is reconsidered every 10 years with the census.
   d) has terms of three years.
   e) All of the above

4) The California State Senate
   a) is based on population, which is reconsidered every 10 years with the census.
   b) has 40 members.
   c) has no Republican women.
   d) has four-year terms.
   e) All of the above

5) The most powerful player in the state legislature is
   a) the speaker of the assembly.
   b) the senate pro tem.
   c) the chair of the Rules Committee.
   d) the majority leader.
   e) the majority whip.

6) California's policy committees
   a) are not particularly important in the senate, because it is a smaller institution; most of the work occurs on the senate floor during debate.
   b) are not open to the public, but the public can submit their concerns in writing to be taken up in committee.
   c) consist of special committees only, formed to review an important issue facing California.
   d) help make the legislative process more manageable, given there are over 7,000 bills proposed a session.
   e) are divided by region.

7) The Legislative Analyst's Office (LAO)
   a) works with the majority party to review the constitutionality of its proposals.
   b) is the liaison to the governor's office to negotiate with the legislature.
   c) is required to sign all bills in order for a bill to become law.
   d) offers nonbinding legislation to counties and cities.
   e) is a nonpartisan office created to provide the legislature with budgetary and fiscal information.

8) The California Legislature
   a) may propose an unlimited amount of bills.
   b) may propose concurrent and joint resolutions and constitutional amendments.
   c) may propose a new law or repeal an existing law.
   d) may repeal popular initiatives that the legislature finds unconstitutional.
   e) B and C only

9) In California, in order for a bill to become law,
   a) it must be submitted to the public, in writing, for review.
   b) it must receive a two-thirds vote in both the assembly and the senate if it spends tax dollars.
   c) it must pass the policy committee by a two-thirds vote.
   d) it must pass the assembly with a positive majority vote.
   e) the governor's approval is not required if a majority of the legislature has approved the bill.

10) The budget bill
   a) is often extremely difficult to pass in the state legislature because of the supermajority required to pass it.
   b) is directed by the state legislature only.
   c) has shared responsibility with the governor, whose item veto is the final say.
   d) is different from the appropriation bill, which reflects the governor's budget.
   e) must be passed by unanimous vote in both chambers.

INTERNET RESOURCES

California Legislature Information: **http://www.leginfo.ca.gov**
California State Assembly: **http://assembly.ca.gov**
Legislative Analyst's Office: **http://lao.ca.gov**
California State Senate: **http://www.sen.ca.gov**

CHAPTER 7: *THE EXECUTIVE BRANCH*

INTRODUCTION

Article V of California's constitution vests supreme executive power in the governor. The Progressive tradition in California has produced a system in which the people vote on an amazing array of politicians and issues. The practice reflects a distrust of government and a resistance to concentrating power in individual officeholders. Both tendencies characterize California's statewide executives; voters elect not only the governor but also a number of functionaries and department heads that would be appointed at the federal level. For example, the administration of justice is a major executive responsibility. The president exercises this power through his appointment of the attorney general, who heads the Department of Justice. In California, however, the attorney general is elected separately and thus remains relatively immune to influence by the governor. To further limit this plural executive, all are subject to limits of two terms of four years each in the same office.

OVERVIEW OF THE GOVERNOR

Term of Office

The governor is elected in a statewide election for a term of four years by the people. The constitution restricts the governor to two terms of office.[56] Governor Schwarzenegger, following the recall election of 2003, was inaugurated as California's thirty-eighth governor, and reelected in 2006 for a full term of office.

Qualifications

There are very few legal requirements to be eligible to serve as governor of California. Under Article V, Section 2 of California's constitution, the qualifications for governor dictate that the governor must be 18 years of age, and have been a citizen of the United States and a resident of California for five years immediately preceding the governor's election. The governor may not hold other public office during his or her tenure as governor.

Compensation

In June 2006, the California Citizens Compensation Commission voted to increase the salaries of California's executives. The governor receives an annual salary of $206,500. The commission has the authority to review and increase the salary levels of the executive officers in the state, including the governor, lieutenant governor, attorney general, controller, treasurer, secretary of state, superintendent of public instruction, insurance commissioner, Board of Equalization members, and members of the state legislature.

---

[56] Article V, Section 2.

Removal

The governor of California may be removed from office through the process of impeachment and removal, or the recall procedure. As discussed in Chapter 6, the impeachment procedure is established in Article IV, Section 18 of the California Constitution. The recall, as discussed in Chapter 4, is the power of the electors to remove an elective officer.

POWERS OF THE GOVERNOR

Informal Powers

Despite sharing power with other independently elected officials, the governor of California is a powerful individual. As political leader of the nation's most populous state, he or she is a national figure who often appears in discussions of presidential and vice presidential hopefuls. Past governors have exerted influence informally in many ways, such as taking strong public stands on issues and sponsoring initiatives such as Proposition 187, the anti-illegal immigrant measure supported by Governor Pete Wilson in 1996, and opposing others such as Proposition 66, an amendment to California's Three Strikes law by Governor Schwarzenegger in 2004. Governor Schwarzenegger suffered a defeat in the November 8, 2005 special election he called personally to advance four ballot initiatives. The election cost taxpayers over $50 million dollars, and none of the initiatives passed.

Formal Powers

In addition to political leadership, the governor has many formal powers, which make him the preeminent player in the legislative process. Like the president of the United States, he or she proposes legislation, particularly in his annual message, the State of the State Address. The governor can call special sessions of the legislature to address a specific issue. He or she has power to veto legislation; in the case of bills that spend money (appropriations measures), he or she has an item veto, which permits the governor to eliminate or reduce some items without having to veto the entire measure.

Budgetary Power. As discussed in Chapter 6, the governor has particular power over the state budget. With the aid of the Department of Finance, the governor prepares the budget and has an item veto over it once it passes the legislature. Most governors do not wait until the budget returns for signature before deciding which parts to sign and which parts to veto. They engage in ongoing negotiations with legislative leaders of both parties. The governor must include the leaders of the minority party because the budget, unlike most bills, must receive support from two-thirds of both houses of the legislature.

This special two-thirds requirement makes California unique among the states, and greatly complicates the process of arriving at a consensus on state spending. In recent years, the assembly has had the most difficulty passing a budget, most likely the result of the turnover created by term limits. Thus, several governors have tended to concentrate on reaching compromises with the senate leadership and then waiting for the assembly to come into line.

78

Appointment Powers. Like the president, the governor has numerous other executive powers. The governor appoints members of hundreds of boards and commissions as well as the leadership of most state executive departments. The secretaries of 11 major state agencies (State and Consumer Services; Business, Transportation, and Housing; Environmental Protection; Child Development and Education; Food and Agriculture; Health and Welfare; Resources; Trade and Commerce; Veterans Affairs; and the Youth and Adult Correctional Agency as well as the Director of Finance, the Director of Industrial Relations, and the Director of Information Technology) comprise the governor's cabinet and serve as the governor's chief policy advisory body. Unlike the president, however, the governor may not appoint the administrative heads of the Department of Justice (attorney general), Department of Education (superintendent of public instruction), or Department of Insurance (insurance commissioner), nor may the governor appoint the state treasurer and controller. The governor plays a role in the selection of judges and fills vacancies on boards of supervisors and other constitutional offices. California's constitution provides that the governor is commander-in-chief of the National Guard and has clemency powers (pardons, reprieves, and commutations) over criminals convicted of violating state laws. He or she also is the authority in extraditions, when another state asks for the return of a criminal who has fled to avoid prosecution or a prison sentence.

Jerry Brown, was elected governor in the November 2, 2010 elections with over 54 percent of the vote. Brown was elected California's governor in 1974 and again in 1978. After serving as Oakland's mayor from 1998-2006, he ran for California's Attorney General and won. Brown's opponent, Meg Whitman, a former eBay executive, was the first female Republican to run for governor. According to the secretary of state's office, Meg Whitman spent almost $107 million on TV and radio advertising compared to Jerry Brown's $21 million; columnist Steve Lopez notes she spent about $50 on each vote she received.[57]

LIEUTENANT GOVERNOR

The lieutenant governor becomes acting governor if the governor dies or otherwise vacates the office. He or she also becomes acting governor any time the governor leaves the state. Like the national vice president, he or she presides over the state senate and may vote in case of a tie. The lieutenant governor also serves on several boards and commissions, including the Board of Regents of the University of California and the Board of Trustees of the California State University system.

Candidates for lieutenant governor run independently of gubernatorial candidates. Indeed, over the last 25 years, governors and lieutenant governors often have been members of different parties. This makes it more difficult for a governor to run nationally for president or vice president since he or she would make a political foe if he or she won.

---

[57] Steve Lopez: "Meg Whitman spent $50 for each vote she got. Is that an outrageous extravagance?" *Los Angeles Times* November 4, 2010

Gavin Newsome, former mayor of San Francisco was elected in November 2010. It is notable that the governor and the lieutenant governor are from same party, which has not always been the case due to California's system of electing executives separately.

ATTORNEY GENERAL

The attorney general is the elected head of the state Department of Justice. The Department of Justice carries out its responsibilities through the following 10 divisions: Division of Civil Law; Division of Public Rights; Division of Criminal Law; Division of Law Enforcement; Division of Gambling Control; California Justice Information Services Division; Division of Legal Support and Technology; Division of Firearms; Executive Division; and Administrative Services Division. The attorney general is both the state's chief prosecutor and the attorney for state officials and agencies when they are defendants. He or she has the general responsibility of enforcing all state and local laws, but leaves most law enforcement and prosecution to local sheriffs and police. If, however, the attorney general believes a local district attorney is not conducting a prosecution appropriately, he or she may intervene and have his office perform that function.

The attorney general is a politically important official who frequently moves up to the governorship. His position in law enforcement gives him visibility second only to the governor's. Kamala Harris was leading in votes as of November 4, 2010 to serve as California's first female attorney general but the vote is still too close to call. She would also be the first African American woman and South Asian American woman in California to serve in this office.

The attorney general represents the people of California in civil and criminal matters before trial courts, appellate courts, and the supreme courts of California and the United States. Therefore, the attorney general's name will appear in court cases representing the state. In a recent case, *Lockyer* v. *Andrade* (2003), the Supreme Court of the United States upheld California's "three strikes" law. The law provides that any felony could constitute the third strike, subjecting an accused person to a prison term of 25 years to life, which the appellants argued is cruel and unusual punishment in violation of the federal Constitution.

SECRETARY OF STATE

The secretary of state is the state's chief elections officer. He or she has the responsibility of certifying when elections will be held and what propositions and offices will appear on the ballot. She also receives and files the records and papers of the state. The secretary of state's office also maintains the Domestic Partners Registry, the Advance Health Care Directive (AHCD) Registry, and the Safe at Home program.[58] The program registers both same-sex couples as well as heterosexual couples in which one partner is at least 62 years old as domestic partners in California. The AHCD program allows unmarried couples to designate health care treatment preferences. Finally, the Safe at Home program provides assistance to victims of "domestic violence, sexual assault, stalking victims and people who work with reproductive health care clinics, enabling these Californians to safely

---

[58] Secretary of State's official Web page: http://www.ss.ca.gov.

receive mail and register to vote while protecting themselves and their children at home and at school."[59] There is little room for policy initiative in the job although the secretary can exert political leadership, such as suggesting legislation or promoting initiatives. The office is a low-profile, administrative position that rarely attracts political attention. Jerry Brown was an exception when he used his promotion of the Political Reform Act to gain attention and eventually the governorship.

Democrat Debra Bowen was reelected in November of 2010. Bowen is the sixth woman in California history to be elected to a statewide constitutional office. She served three full terms in the assembly before moving to the senate, in which she served two terms before running for secretary of state. She replaced Bruce McPherson, who was appointed by Governor Schwarzenegger in March 2005 to replace Kevin Shelly, who resigned in 2005 under state and federal investigations for misspent voting funds and for receiving illegal campaign contributions.

CONTROLLER

The controller is the state's chief fiscal officer. He or she keeps track of the state's finances and pays most of its bills. The controller also has the authority to audit state executive departments. The controller chairs the state's two most important tax administration agencies: the Franchise Tax Board, which collects state income taxes, and the Board of Equalization, which collects the sales tax and equalizes property taxes between counties.

The controller is usually a low-profile official although former controller Gray Davis moved from there to the office of lieutenant governor to become the governor in 1998.

John Chiang, a Democrat, was reelected to serve as Controller in November 2010.

TREASURER

The treasurer frequently is described as the state's banker. He or she invests surplus state funds, not only when a budget surplus exists, but also when the state has temporarily collected more tax dollars than it immediately needs to pay its bills. It is the responsibility of the treasurer to prepare, sell, and redeem state bonds. The people must vote to authorize these bonds (Chapter 2), but the treasurer has the flexibility to time the actual sale to maximize the state's credit rating and minimize the interest rate. The treasurer is also a member of the board of the state's two big pension plans: PERS, the Public Employees Retirement System, and STRS, the State Teachers Retirement System. In this capacity, he or she has an important influence on how the pension funds of teachers and state and local employees are invested. Due to the size of the funds, the treasurer is also a major factor in the U.S. financial markets.

On the surface, the treasurer's job appears to be primarily administrative, but it is an office that can attract substantial campaign funds from bond brokers, bankers, and others

---

[59] Secretary of State's official Web page: http://www.ss.ca.gov.

with a stake in the disposition of state monies. For example, Matt Fong used the office as a platform for becoming the Republican nominee for the U.S. Senate in 1998.

Bill Lockyer, a Democrat, is the former state attorney general, and was reelected to serve as treasurer of California. In addition to his executive branch offices, Lockyer served for 25 years in the California State Legislature.

SUPERINTENDENT OF PUBLIC INSTRUCTION

The superintendent of public instruction represents an unusual arrangement. The public elects this person head of the state Department of Education under the direction of the Board of Education, a 10-member body appointed by the governor. In other words, the appointed board makes policy while administration is the responsibility of the elected official. In practice, the advantage of being publicly elected usually helps the superintendent to maintain primary influence over K-12 educational policy in the state.

The superintendent of public instruction is the only statewide official elected on a nonpartisan ballot. Since more than one-third of the state budget flows through this department, most of it to local districts and programs, the state board and the superintendent exercise substantial power, but not always in harmony. Moreover, the influence of the superintendent has been in decline in recent years because the governor has created an appointive office, the secretary of education, to advise him and publicly promote his education agenda.

Tom Torlakson was elected to serve as superintendent of public instruction in November 2010.

INSURANCE COMMISSIONER

The insurance commissioner is the administrative head of the state Department of Insurance. This agency licenses and regulates insurance companies, agents, and brokers who wish to operate in the state. The commissioner must review and approve rate increases for various types of insurance, following a public hearing if the proposals exceed certain percentage increases.

Prior to 1988, the governor appointed the insurance commissioner. In that year, however, the people approved Proposition 103, which made the position elective. The job is a rather technical one, which was probably better left to appointment, but it is typical of Progressive California to spread power among numerous elected officials.

Dave Jones was elected to his first term as insurance commissioner in November 2010.

BOARD OF EQUALIZATION

The Board of Equalization consists of four members elected in huge districts, and a fifth member, the state controller. The board collects and administers state and local sales and use taxes. It also collects any excise taxes, such as those on tobacco and alcohol.

Originally established to equalize property taxes for public utilities that had property in more than one county, today it may also review each county's tax assessment procedures.

POLITICS UNUSUAL: GOVERNOR GRAY DAVIS

With his election to the office in 1998, and reelection in 2002, Democratic governor Gray Davis had proven himself to be an amazingly successful fundraiser and campaigner. He survived rolling blackouts and skyrocketing energy costs following the energy deregulation policies implemented between 2000 and 2001, and was dealing with an economic slowdown that was threatening a budget deficit in the range of $30 to 35 billion unless drastic cuts were made in state and local programs and taxes raised in record dollar amounts. Some would say Davis was lucky; Davis' luck ran out on October 7, 2003, when the recall election ousted the career California politician.

Davis brought a lifetime of political experience to the job. He was first elected to the assembly in 1982 and subsequently held the office of controller and lieutenant governor. Prior to his election to the assembly, he served as former governor Jerry Brown's chief of staff. Davis was a consummate state capitol insider.

Despite the fact that his legislative and other political experience should have taught him basic tactfulness, Davis got off on the wrong foot, when, following his elevation to the governorship, he declared that the job of the legislature was to "implement my vision." It was no surprise that the legislature reacted testily to this pronouncement. While it is not unusual for governors to feud with legislatures controlled by the opposing party, Davis had a history of contentious relationships with a legislature that has been safely in the hands of his Democratic Party.

For example, the historic average veto rate for California governors is 7 percent, yet Davis vetoed over 22 percent of the bills that reached his desk. He also had highly public disagreements with the lieutenant governor, Democrat Cruz Bustamante over affirmative action policy as well as with both a former Democratic state controller and his appointed chair of the Public Utilities Commission over energy policy. Capitol insiders say that he has a mercurial temper. Voters viewed him as cold and aloof.

But he had never lost an election. One reason is that he was the most successful fundraiser in state history, and money is essential to winning California elections. During his first six months in office he raked in $6.1 million—approximately $225,000 per week. While defeating multimillionaire Republican candidate Bill Simon in 2002, he spent over $72 million, twice that of his opponent, but won by only a 47 percent to 42 percent margin. Some commentators note that he had been very, very lucky in facing opponents with modest qualifications and inept campaign strategies.

One may wonder whether Davis would have lost his job if Arnold Schwarzenegger, a hugely popular movie star and successful businessman, had not been a candidate for replacing the ousted governor. Support for firing the governor met with mixed emotions following the Ninth Circuit's full review of its decision to postpone the election, indicating that Davis's job was most threatened by the popular appeal of Schwarzenegger. No other replacement candidate captured the attention of the electorate.

SCHWARZENEGGER'S GOVERNORSHIP

Opinion polls during the summer of 2005, nearly two years after his election with soaring public approval ratings, indicated that Schwarzenegger was performing about as well as his predecessor, with 58 percent of Californians disapproving of his job performance and a 31 percent approval rate.[60] However, it was evident that Schwarzenegger was headed for trouble after the defeat of every proposition on the 2005 special election ballot, four of which were his own. Despite the slide in his favorability following the special election, Schwarzenegger bounced back with a promise of better relations with the legislature and more bipartisanship behavior. His reelection in November 2006 is testimony to the good graces the voters gave him. However, at the close of his second term, the voters have not held onto these warm feelings. According to the PPIC survey in October 2010, 28 percent of Californians approve of the governor's job performance while 65 percent disapprove (the remaining answered don't know). Even Republicans had unfavorable ratings for the governor with only 30 percent approval among Republicans. This is a considerable drop from the high of 65 percent in August 2004.

SOMETHING TO THINK ABOUT

1. In what ways does the governor have more power over the state budget than the legislature?

2. How have legislative term limits impacted the powers and responsibilities of the governor?

3. How has the initiative process changed the potential power of the governor?

4. How did the recall election impact Californians' view of government?

5. What challenges does the independence of California's executive departments present for California's government?

6. What are the advantages to a plural executive? What are the disadvantages?

MULTIPLE-CHOICE QUESTIONS

1) The Progressive tradition is evident in California's executive branch because
   a) Californians trust the governor to execute the business of the government.
   b) the governor has the power to appoint department heads.
   c) the attorney general has the power to represent cases in court.
   d) voters elect functionaries and department heads.
   e) the executive positions are subject to the governor.

---

[60]Robert Salladay and Evan Halper, "As Popularity Ebbs, Governor Reaches Out." *Los Angeles Times*, June 22, 2005.

2) The California Citizens Compensation Commission
   a) gives advice to the governor with regard to the other executive departments.
   b) determines the salaries of the executives in California's government.
   c) appoints members to the Board of Equalization.
   d) ensures that executives are not working at other jobs while they are in office.
   e) once refused to give the members of the executive branch a raise until they passed a budget.

3) The governor's powers include
   a) proposing legislation.
   b) veto of bills.
   c) include item veto of budget items.
   d) include serving as the figurehead of the state.
   e) All of the above

4) With regard to initiatives,
   a) governors are forbidden from taking a political stance.
   b) governors are allowed to take a stance but are forbidden to sponsor an initiative.
   c) several governors have bypassed the legislature to enact laws through direct democracy.
   d) in the past 15 years, governors have been less likely to use the initiative.
   e) they do not help the governor get his agenda passed because the legislature can override his veto.

5) The lieutenant governor
   a) is the president of the senate.
   b) takes over for the governor in his absence or incapacity.
   c) serves on the Board of Regents of the University of California and the Board of Trustees of the California State University system.
   d) B and C only
   e) All of the above

6) The attorney general carries out his or her duties through
   a) 10 divisions that handle issues, including gambling, firearms, criminal law, civil law, and public rights.
   b) local law enforcement, including police and sheriffs.
   c) assigning cases to district attorneys based on subject matter.
   d) 10 deputies elected separately to handle issues, including gambling, firearms, criminal law, civil law, and public rights.
   e) local city attorneys based on the subject matter.

7) The elected executive in charge of the Domestic Partners Registry is the
   a) lieutenant governor.
   b) attorney general.
   c) controller.
   d) governor.
   e) secretary of state.

8) The _____ is the state's chief fiscal officer.
   a) secretary of state
   b) treasurer
   c) lieutenant governor
   d) controller
   e) attorney general

9) The _____ prepares, sells, and redeems state bonds, as well as invests surplus funds.
   a) secretary of state
   b) treasurer
   c) lieutenant governor
   d) controller
   e) attorney general

10) The superintendent of public instruction
   a) makes policy for the Department of Education.
   b) administers the business of the Department of Education.
   c) is elected on the partisan ballot just like the other executive officers.
   d) works with 10 other members of the Board of Education, who are elected by region.
   e) All of the above

INTERNET SOURCES

The Governor and Statewide Offices: **http://www.ca.gov**
Lieutenant Governor's Homepage: **http://www.ltg.ca.gov**
California Secretary of State: **http://www.ss.ca.gov**
Attorney General's Homepage: **http://www.ag.ca.gov**
California Department of Justice, Office of the Attorney General: **http://caag.state.ca.us**
*California State Treasurer's Homepage: **http://www.ag.ca.gov***
*State Controller's Homepage: **http://www.sco.ca.gov***
Insurance Commissioner's Homepage: **http://www.insurance.ca.gov**
*California Department of Education: **http://www.cde.ca.gov***
*California Department of Corrections and Rehabilitation: **http://www.cya.ca.gov/***
*California Energy Commission: **http://www.energy.ca.gov***

86

CHAPTER 8: *THE COURTS AND THE JUDICIAL SYSTEM*

INTRODUCTION

The California courts are established as courts of record in Article VI of the California Constitution. In a court of record, proceedings are kept as a permanent official record. California's court system is the largest in the nation; it employs over 2,000 judicial officers, 19,000 court employees, and hears nearly 9 million cases, serving over 34 million people. The state constitution vests the judicial power of California in the supreme court, courts of appeal, and superior courts. The constitution also provides for the formation and functions of the Judicial Council, the policymaking body for the state courts and other agencies.[61]

California's courts handle matters of both civil and criminal law, providing for the orderly settlement of disputes between parties in controversy; determining the guilt or innocence of those who are accused of violating the laws; settling the estates of deceased persons; performing judicial review; and protecting the rights of individuals from encroachment by state or local government.[62]

STRUCTURE OF THE COURTS

Like the federal courts, California's courts are divided into two jurisdictions: trial courts and appellate courts. Trial courts are the fact-finding courts because their jobs are to determine the facts of a case; this may include determining whether a crime occurred (criminal court) or settling disputes between two parties or individuals, like whether a person is responsible for damaging another's property (civil court). These courts have original jurisdiction; this means that they will be the first court to hear a case. The courts of appeal, which include the California Supreme Court, review questions of law and due process and have appellate jurisdiction, hearing cases on appeal, or in certain cases may have original jurisdiction. Jurisdiction here refers to the authority of a court to interpret and apply the law. Since this is progressive California, where the people vote on a wide array of issues and officials, it is noteworthy that even judges' names are submitted to California voters for approval.

SUPERIOR COURTS

Superior courts are the trial courts or fact-finding courts in California. They are established in each of the 58 counties in more than 450 locations, with about 1,498 judges to deal with both civil and criminal matters. Civil disputes occur when citizens or legal entities sue each other, either for damages (usually money) or to prevent harm or irreparable damage; criminal cases involve violation of criminal laws, ranging from minor infractions, such as jaywalking, to serious felonies, such as murder. Juries are commonly used in superior court.

---

[61] Fact Sheet: California Judicial Branch, February 2005.
[62] The Judicial Department California's Legislature, http://www.leginfo.ca.gov/pdf/caleg5.pdf.

There are several specialized subdivisions of superior courts. Traffic court deals with all traffic violations except those committed by juveniles. Small claims court is where citizens or legal entities may sue each other if the amount involved is $7,500 or less. Small claims courts do not use lawyers or juries. There is a limit on the number of times an individual may sue under the system in any given year. There is no limit on the number of claims an individual who seeks less than $2,500 may file, but California law limits to two the number of claims a person may file over $2,500.

California established other subdivisions of the courts to deal with inheritance and probate, families, and juveniles. Probate court involves the administration of wills and estates. Family law courts settle domestic disputes; they are concerned with divorce and child custody. Juvenile courts deal with matters affecting accused persons under the age of 18 years. An exception occurs when prosecutors choose to try young individuals accused of particularly heinous crimes as adults. There are no juries in juvenile proceedings. If punishment includes incarceration, juveniles are sent to the California Youth Authority (CYA).

Superior court judges are elected countywide on a nonpartisan ballot for six-year terms. Vacancies are filled through appointment by the governor. Candidates must be attorneys who have been members of the California bar for 10 years. Joining the bar involves passing a difficult written test as well as being of good character. In order to avoid cluttering the ballot, the name of an unopposed incumbent does not appear. If a vacancy occurs between elections, the governor may appoint a qualified replacement who must then be voted on by the electorate at the next general election. When the workload of a court exceeds the capacity of the existing staff, the judges may appoint attorneys to serve as temporary judges, called commissioners.

During 2006–2007, there were 9,458,064 filings, and 7,886,912 dispositions. Of these, 7,817,052 were criminal filings, 6,446,615 criminal dispositions.1,461,111 civil filings, and 1,286,517civil dispositions.[63]

According to the Judicial Council of California's October 29, 2008 press release, filings are now at their highest level in more than a decade and a half. Since 2001–2002, total filings in the trial courts have grown by a cumulative total of 12 percent, an increase of over a million filings. This figure includes misdemeanor and infractions filings, increasing by 16 and 20 percent, respectively, in the last five years. Felony filings are up by 12 percent in the last five years. Finally, juvenile delinquency filings declined slightly last year but have grown by 10 percent over the last five years.

COURTS OF APPEAL AND THE SUPREME COURT

Trial courts decide questions of fact: did the accused kill the victim? Appellate courts decide questions of procedure or law: were the rights of the accused violated by the police during their questioning? Does California's law violate an individual's guarantee of free speech? California has two levels of appellate courts: the courts of appeal and the state supreme court.

---

[63] 2008 Court Statistics Report Statewide Caseload Trends 2006-2007, Judicial Council of California.

In 1904, California voters approved a legislative amendment to Article VI of the California Constitution to create intermediate appellate courts to help alleviate court congestion confronting the California Supreme Court. The amendment also provided that beginning with the 1906 election, the justices would be elected.

Today, California has six district courts of appeal, with 105 justices serving in the courts. The districts are detailed in Figure 8:1. Each court includes a number of justices who sit in a panel of three to hear appeals from superior courts or certain state agencies. Decisions of the panels (opinions) are published in the California Appellate Reports. Opinions will be published if they establish a new rule of law, involve a legal issue of continuing public interest, criticize existing law, or make a significant contribution to legal literature.[64] Each of the six courts selects one of its members to be the presiding justice, who is the administrative head of the court. The six courts are located in San Diego (with divisions in Riverside and Santa Ana), Los Angeles (with a division in Ventura), Fresno, San Jose, San Francisco, and Sacramento.

Courts of appeal have both appellate jurisdiction (hearing appeals) and original jurisdiction (first court to hear a case). Like the supreme court, the courts of appeal have original jurisdiction in *habeas corpus*, *mandamus*, *certiorari*, and prohibition proceedings.[65] Generally, a criminal or civil defendant who loses in superior court has the right to appeal to the court of appeals for a reversal of the decision. In civil cases, however, if a party appeals a monetary award and loses, interest will be added to the amount to cover the extra time consumed on appeal.

Between 2006 and 2007, there were 24,934 filings in the courts of appeal including 15,527 notices of appeal and 9,407 original proceedings. This includes 6,508 criminal cases, 6,116 civil cases, and 2,903 juvenile cases.[66]

---

[64] 2008 Court Statistics Report Statewide Caseload Trends 2006-2007, Judicial Council of California
[65] California Constitution, Article VI, Section 10.
[66] 2008 Court Statistics Report Statewide Caseload Trends 2006-2007, Judicial Council of California.

Figure 8:1 – CALIFORNIA COURTS OF APPEAL

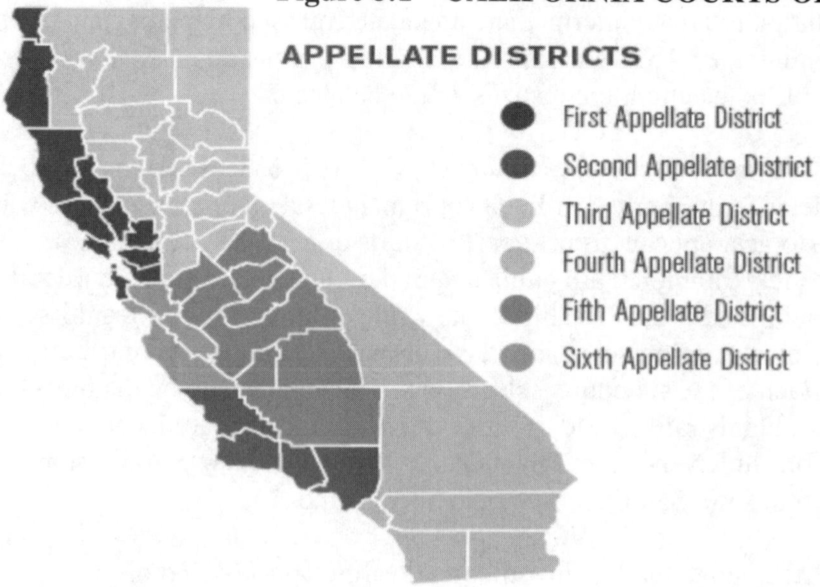

APPELLATE DISTRICTS

- First Appellate District
- Second Appellate District
- Third Appellate District
- Fourth Appellate District
- Fifth Appellate District
- Sixth Appellate District

Source: California Appellate
Court Visitor's Guide 2006

CALIFORNIA SUPREME COURT

The Supreme Court of California is the state's highest court. Its decisions are binding on all other California courts. The court conducts regular sessions in San Francisco, Los Angeles, and Sacramento; it also occasionally holds special sessions elsewhere.

Jurisdiction

The court has original jurisdiction in a few cases (meaning it is the first to hear the charges), but most of its work is appellate. The cases it reviews are usually decided in superior court, then acted on by a court of appeals. In most cases, the supreme court may decide which cases it chooses to hear. In cases where the death penalty has been imposed, however, the convicted person has the right to appeal the sentence to the supreme court. In all cases, the decision by the court is final unless the U.S. Supreme Court finds a constitutional issue in the case. The supreme court has original jurisdiction in proceedings for extraordinary relief in the form of *mandamus*, *certiorari*, and prohibition. The court also has original jurisdiction in *habeas corpus* proceedings.

The state constitution gives the supreme court the authority to review decisions of the state courts of appeal. This reviewing power enables the supreme court to decide important legal questions and to maintain uniformity in the law. The court selects specific issues for review, or it may decide all the issues in a case. There were 9,247 filings recorded in the California Supreme Court in 2006–2007. This is an increase from the prior period, as Figure 8:1 details. While a sharp increase occurred in the latter part of the 1990s, more recently the number of appeals filed to the Supreme Court has leveled off.

90

During that same period, the Supreme Court issued 113 written opinions and filed 17 automatic appeals arising out of judgments of death in 2006–2007.[67] All decisions of the Supreme Court are issued in writing and made public. The court's opinions are made accessible in various ways, including publication in the *Official California Reports.*

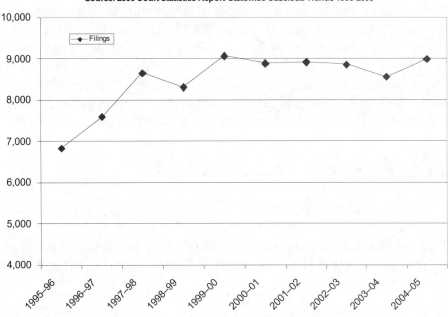

Figure 8:2 California Supreme Court Filings 1995-2005
Source: 2006 Court Statistics Report-Statewide Caseload Trends 1995-2005

In addition, the California Supreme Court reviews reports of the Commission on Judicial Performance and the State Bar of California regarding investigations of misconduct and recommendations for discipline of judges and attorneys. The Supreme Court also hears appeals from decisions of the Public Utilities Commission.

Membership and Qualifications

The California Supreme Court is composed of seven justices: a chief justice, who is appointed specifically to that position, and six associate justices. Justices of both the courts of appeals and the supreme court are selected by a complex process. First, the governor forwards the names of potential justices to the Commission on Judicial Nominee Evaluation (JNE). This 25-member commission includes 19 members elected by the bar, which is the association of attorneys admitted to the practice of law in California. The other six are public members appointed by the governor. This commission considers the qualifications, including the character, of each proposed nominee, and rates him or her exceptionally well-qualified, well-qualified, qualified, or unqualified. Only on the rare occasions when the governor disregards the rating and nominates a person ranked unqualified is the rating made public.

---

[67] 2008 Court Statistics Report Statewide Caseload Trends 2006-2007, Judicial Council of California

91

After the governor receives the ratings of the JNE, he or she chooses who to nominate to either the supreme court or one of the six courts of appeal. The governor sends this nomination to the Commission on Judicial Appointments. This commission is composed of the chief justice of the state supreme court (or an associate justice if the vacancy is the office of chief justice), the senior (longest serving) presiding justice of the court of appeals, and the attorney general. The commission holds public hearings and receives testimony about the nominee in both oral and written form from anyone who wishes to submit it. The three then vote. If two vote to confirm the appointment, the nominee becomes a justice and takes his or her place on the bench. The new justice is either confirmed or rejected by the electorate at the next election, running unopposed. If a majority of the voters affirm the selection, the justice serves the rest of the 12-year term, after which the voters again voice their opinion during a general election. If a majority votes no, the office becomes vacant and the process begins again. Judges are removable through recall as well. In 1986, a move to recall Chief Justice Rose Bird and several others failed, but Justice Bird later lost a confirmation election.

JANICE ROGERS BROWN: SUCCESS STORY

Like most governors, former governor Pete Wilson received recommendations for judicial appointments from many sources. Usually, a judicial appointment secretary in the governor's office processed these suggestions. In some cases, however, the nominee was known personally to the governor. This sometimes led to an unusual effort to ensure the selection.

Janice Brown had worked for Governor Wilson prior to her nomination to the court of appeal. The Commission on Judicial Appointments unanimously confirmed her to that position, but trouble arose when the governor proposed to elevate her to the state supreme court a year and a half later. The Commission on Judicial Nominee Evaluation rated her unqualified to serve on the top court.

The case was a subject of much controversy. Opponents of Justice Brown cited her limited experience at the appellate level as reason for concern. Her defenders suggested that liberal opponents in the bar sought to reject her because she was a conservative black female. The governor, who knew her well, defied the JNE and nominated her anyway.

The resolution of the controversy was actually quite simple politically. The chief justice who voted was a Wilson appointee. The senior presiding justice came from the court of appeals on which Justice Brown had served and supported her. The Attorney General was conservative Republican Dan Lungren. She was confirmed unanimously in a rare rejection of a commission recommendation.

As for Wilson's choice, President Bush nominated Justice Brown to the U.S. Circuit Court of Appeals for the District of Columbia, and she was confirmed on June 8, 2005. The Supreme Court may act in any case with the concurrence of four justices. In cases in which oral argument has already been heard, an opinion may be filed with less than a seven-member court so long as four justices concur in the result. If additional oral arguments are heard before a new supreme court justice is appointed and confirmed, a court of appeals justice will be assigned temporarily to participate in each case, pursuant to the court's established rotational assignment policy.[68]

Governor Gray Davis appointed just one associate justice to the supreme court: Carlos Moreno, historically only the third Latino to serve on the court. Davis has been fairly blunt in stating publicly what all governors think privately. He said, "My appointees should reflect my views."

The newest justice to California's Supreme Court is Associate Justice Carol A. Corrigan, who was appointed in December 2005 and confirmed January 4, 2006. The California Supreme Court is becoming more diverse, as Justice Corrigan brings the number of female justices on California's Supreme Court to three.

OTHER PLAYERS

District Attorneys.

The judicial system includes many other important participants. District attorneys prosecute cases in superior courts. They are elected in each county on a countywide, nonpartisan ballot. Their offices include numerous deputy district attorneys who actually prosecute virtually all the cases.

Public Defenders.

Public defenders are appointed by the county boards of supervisors to defend the accused in a criminal case when he or she cannot afford a private attorney. At times, there is an insufficient number of public defenders available, so the court appoints a private attorney to provide legal services.

Probation Departments.

Counties also have probation departments, which perform evaluations of defendants for the trial courts and supervise those who are put on probation instead of paying fines or going to jail. Generally, probation is an alternative to jail; however, probation is rescinded should a defendant violate the terms the judge specifies.

THE JURY SYSTEM

Trial by a jury of one's peers is among the fundamental democratic ideals of our nation protected in the federal Bill of Rights in both criminal (Sixth Amendment) and civil (Seventh Amendment) trials. Juries are convened to review facts and make decisions in legal proceedings. Juries were established as a mechanism for citizens to oppose an oppressive government.

---

[68] June 20, 2005, "Justice Brown to Leave Supreme Court June 30; Procedures Clarified for High Court Actions," Press Release Judicial Council of California

Grand Juries

Grand juries are convened annually in each county to decide if a suspect should be formally charged with a crime, known as an indictment. However, grand juries are used for broader purposes as well. The three major areas of responsibility of the grand jury include: 1) criminal indictments based on the grand jury's determination if a crime has been committed and there is enough evidence to charge; 2) to accuse public officials of improper actions in performing official duties; 3) to serve as watchdog of local government under its civil law responsibilities. Under California law, grand juries in counties with a population of over 4 million have 23 members; other counties have 19.[69] In order for a criminal grand jury to issue an indictment or an accusation, it needs at least 12 of the 19 grand jurors, or 15 of the 23-member jury to approve.

In California, as in most states, methods used for grand jury selection do not provide for a cross section of the community. Those chosen tend to be older, better educated, and more affluent than the community at large. Women and minorities tend to be underrepresented, which may pose legal problems in criminal indictments. However, for criminal indictments, some California counties select special grand juries from the regular, petit jury, rolls.[70]

Petit (Trial) Juries

California responded to calls for change to its jury system and created the Blue Ribbon Commission on Jury System Improvement in 1995 to review ways to improve jury service. Since then, California's courts have made many efforts to improve jury service. California has adopted "a one-day-or-one-trial" system in which a juror reporting for service either is assigned to a trial on the first day or is dismissed from service for at least 12 months. The majority of jurors serve for just one day, and of those selected for a trial, most complete their service within one week. Failure to report for jury service in California may result in a fine up to $1,500, and it is possible to face jail time in addition to the fine. It is against the law for an employer to prevent an employee from serving on a jury by threatening to fire or terminating employment on that basis. California pays jurors $15 a day, and reimburses them at least 34 cents per mile starting on the second day of service.

To serve on a jury in the state of California, a person must be an elector, which includes U.S. citizenship, and must be at least 18 years old. In addition, jurors must be able to understand English enough to understand and discuss the case; a resident of the county in which the summons was delivered; have completed prior jury service more than 12 months preceding; and not be serving currently on a grand jury or on another trial jury. A person who is in prison or on parole is ineligible for jury service.

---

[69] Dr. Marianne Jameson, California Grand Jurors Association, *The Grand Jury: A Brief Historical Overview*
[70] Dr. Marianne Jameson, California Grand Jurors Association, *The Grand Jury: A Brief Historical Overview*

The jury pool is drawn from voter Department of Motor Vehicles registration and voter registration lists. Once selected for a case, jurors may be subjected to *voir dire*, an examination by the prosecution (or plaintiff, in a civil case) and defense (respondent) to determine whether a prospective juror may not be able to objectively hear a case. Both the judge and the lawyer may excuse individual jurors from service in a particular case for various reasons. Lawyers use a "challenge" to excuse a juror; challenges can be for cause or peremptory. A lawyer has an unlimited number of challenges for cause, but a limited number of peremptory challenges, which require no reason to exercise. Lawyers for both sides are entitled 10 peremptory challenges in criminal cases, 20 in death penalty cases, and six in civil cases.[71]

Once seated, during a trial, jurors cannot discuss the case with anyone until deliberations begin. They are required to hear all evidence presented and are prohibited from pursuing an independent investigation of the case. During deliberations, jurors must consider only information and evidence presented in the courtroom. If the jury is not able to agree on a verdict, the judge may dismiss the jury as a "hung jury" and call for a mistrial. This also may mean the case will go to trial again with a new jury.

STATE BAR OF CALIFORNIA

Many students wishing to practice law hear stories about the "Bar" exam. According to the Fact Sheet issued by the Judicial Council of California, the State Bar of California is a public corporation, established within Article VI of the California Constitution. The bar is the "administrative arm of the Supreme Court in matters of attorney admission and discipline." It is most well-known for the Committee of Bar Examiners who administer the bar examination and other requirements for admission to the practice of law and certifies qualified applicants to the Supreme Court for admission.

SOMETHING TO THINK ABOUT

1. What are the advantages and disadvantages to the various methods of judicial selection in California?

2. How does California's judiciary compare to the federal judicial structure?

3. What are the effects of election terms for judges in California?

4. How has California improved its jury system? What are some of the criticisms and challenges to California's jury system?

5. How does California's multicultural and multiethnic population affect California's judicial system?

---

[71] California Code of Civil Procedure, sec. 231

MULTIPLE-CHOICE QUESTIONS

1) Fact finding for disputes between private parties or individuals would be handled by which court?
   a) Civil
   b) Criminal
   c) Appellate
   d) Supreme
   e) None of the above

2) Superior courts have _____ jurisdiction, which means they will be the _____ to hear a case.
   a) appellate; second
   b) superior; second
   c) original; first
   d) appellate; first
   e) supreme; second

3) Superior courts are responsible for
   a) small claims.
   b) determining questions of constitutional law.
   c) criminal cases only.
   d) civil cases only.
   e) fact finding.

4) Superior court judges
   a) are appointed by the governor.
   b) are elected countywide on a nonpartisan ballot.
   c) are elected statewide on a nonpartisan ballot.
   d) are elected countywide on a partisan ballot.
   e) are elected statewide on a partisan ballot.

5) There are _____ California courts of appeal.
   a) two
   b) four
   c) six
   d) eight
   e) None of the above

6) An appellate court opinion will be published if
   a) it establishes a new rule of law.
   b) it involves a legal issue of continuing public interest.
   c) it criticizes an existing law.
   d) it makes a significant contribution to legal literature.
   e) All of the above

7) With regard to caseload, the supreme court of California generally _____, but in _____ cases, the defendant has an automatic appeal.
   a) has original jurisdiction; death penalty
   b) must hear each case that has been appealed unless the court votes not to hear it; civil
   c) chooses which cases to hear; death penalty
   d) chooses which cases to hear; civil
   e) has appellate jurisdiction; civil

8) There are ____ justices on California's supreme court; these justices must be ____.
   a) seven; confirmed by the voters after nomination and confirmation has been made by the governor and the Commission on Judicial Appointments, respectively
   b) nine; nominated by the governor and confirmed by the Commission on Judicial Nominee Evaluation
   c) six; confirmed by the Commission on Judicial Nominee Evaluation after nomination by the voters
   d) seven; nominated by the governor and confirmed by the Commission on Judicial Nominee Evaluation
   e) nine; confirmed by the voters after the initial nomination has been made by the governor

9) District attorneys
   a) are elected countywide and defend the accused in a criminal case when he or she cannot afford a private attorney.
   b) are appointed countywide and prosecute cases in the appellate courts.
   c) are elected statewide and perform evaluations of defendants for the trial courts.
   d) are appointed countywide and prosecute cases in superior court.
   e) are elected countywide and prosecute cases in superior court.

10) All of the following statements about grand juries are true EXCEPT
   a) they convene annually to decide on criminal indictments.
   b) they determine whether a crime has been committed and if there is enough evidence to charge.
   c) they determine whether a defendant is guilty or not guilty.
   d) they accuse public officials of improper actions in the course of performing official duties.
   e) they serve as a watchdog of local government under its civil law responsibilities.

INTERNET SOURCES

California Courts Online Self-Help Center: **http://www.courtinfo.ca.gov/selfhelp/**
Information on Jury Duty in California: **http://www.courtinfo.ca.gov/jury/index.htm**
California Appellate Courts Opinions: **http://www.courtinfo.ca.gov/opinions/**
California Courts Programs Homepage: **http://www.courtinfo.ca.gov/programs/**
California Court Administration: **http://www.courtinfo.ca.gov/courtadmin/**
California Rules of Court: **http://www.courtinfo.ca.gov/rules/**
The State Bar of California: **http://www.calbar.ca.gov/state/calbar/calbar_home.jsp**

CHAPTER 9: *PUBLIC POLICY IN CALIFORNIA*

INTRODUCTION

Public policies are plans for government action to address social problems, counter threats to public safety and security, or pursue generally accepted objectives. They resolve questions of "who gets what, when, and how."[72] Public policy attempts to do at least one or more of the following: 1) reconcile conflicting claims on scarce resources; 2) establish incentives for cooperation and collective action that would be irrational without government influence; 3) prohibit morally unacceptable behavior; 4) protect the activity of a group or individual, promoting activities that are essential to government; 5) provide direct benefits to citizens.[73] In California, policies are passed by the legislature as statutory laws, by the people through initiatives, by the executive branch through regulations, and by the courts as rulings on existing California laws and regulations.

ECONOMIC POLICY

State and local governments receive revenue from a complex variety of sources. They then spend it on an even greater array of programs and services for their constituents. In Progressive California, there have also been a number of restrictions enacted by the voters through the initiative process. The process is even more complicated by grants California receives from the federal government in order to implement programs and policies the United States Congress has passed. This money is distributed to California and directed towards a variety of services, including welfare, health care, education, homeland security, and particularly for California, a border state, immigration.

THE STATE BUDGET

The governor of California is responsible for preparing the state's budget. This budget contains a projection of expected revenues and a plan for spending those dollars. The governor sets priorities and ultimately must approve the document. Actual preparation is a function of the Department of Finance, headed by a director of finance, who is appointed by the governor. The department works with other state agencies to determine their needs and then submits a draft to the governor. The governor refines the draft and presents it to the legislature in January. The projections of income and expenditure must balance since California may not have a budget deficit. Under state law, the legislature is supposed to return a completed budget to the governor by June 15. A two-thirds vote of both houses is required for passage. The governor then has until July 1, the start of the new fiscal year, to sign it or dissect it with the item veto. Since there is no penalty, this deadline is frequently ignored. For example, the budget for 2011 was not passed until October 8, far surpassing the September 23 passage for the 2009 budget setting a modern record for late approval.

---

[72] Lasswell, H. D. 1936. *Politics: Who Gets What, When, How*. New York: McGraw-Hill.
[73] Theodoulou, Stella Z. and Matthew A. Cahn, 1994. *Public Policy: The Essential Readings*. Prentice Hall.

Income

The state derives its income from a few large and many small sources. The state's revenue sources are illustrated in Figure 9:1. In the budget, over 40 percent of the state's revenue is projected to come from personal income tax. Like the federal government, the state taxes the personal incomes of its citizens. The rate varies from 1 percent of the lowest income to 9.3 percent of the largest. The tax is collected by the Franchise Tax Board, which is chaired by the state controller. The income from this source is highly volatile, because it taxes more heavily the incomes of wealthier persons whose fortunes fluctuate with the stock market.

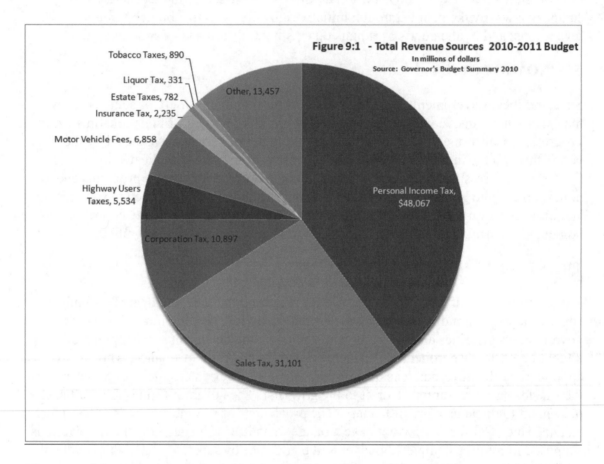

Figure 9:1 - Total Revenue Sources 2010-2011 Budget
In millions of dollars
Source: Governor's Budget Summary 2010

Tobacco Taxes, 890
Liquor Tax, 331
Estate Taxes, 782
Insurance Tax, 2,235
Motor Vehicle Fees, 6,858
Highway Users Taxes, 5,534
Corporation Tax, 10,897
Other, 13,457
Personal Income Tax, $48,067
Sales Tax, 31,101

The second-largest source of state income is the sales tax. This is expected to account for just over 26 percent of the governor's 2010-2011 budget. The Board of Equalization collects a 7.25 percent tax on retail transactions in California. The cities and counties receive 1.5 percent, county transit programs receive 0.25 percent, and the state keeps the rest. Counties may add an additional tax of up to 1.25 percent for projects the state approves, such as parks. They are permitted to keep those dollars.

After the personal income and sales taxes, revenue drops off steeply. The 2010-2011 proposed budgets include 9 percent from bank and corporation taxes, 5.7 percent from motor vehicle taxes, 4.6 percent from the highway users' tax, and other income from

100

numerous minor sources. Table 9:1 details the sources and amounts from a variety of sources in California's budget.

Expenditures

Education is by far the largest category of state expenditures. In years past, K-12 education accounted for the highest percent of expenditures; however, it is evident times have been rough for Californians. The 2010-2011 budget allocates 29.4 percent of the general fund for K–12 education, a nearly 3 percent decrease from the previous year. Another 10.08 percent is slated to go to higher education, which is about the same from the previous year which saw a reduction of nearly 2 percent; this allocation includes the community colleges, the California State University system, and the University of California. Health and human services accounts for 30.08 percent, a slight increase from the previous year. Business, transportation, and housing is slated to receive 9.98 percent of the budget; the legislative, judicial, and executive branches of government will receive 5.16 percent a slight increase from the previous year. This year's budget devotes just under 1.2 percent to environmental protection, and less than half a percent (0.35 percent) to labor and workforce development. As Table 9:1 indicates there are several sources of funding for the various programs California implements. Figure 9:2 illustrates the state's expenditures for 2010-2011.[74]

Table 9:1 Expenditures for General, Special, & Bond Funds, California Budget 2010–2011 (in millions)			
	General Fund	Special Funds	Bond Funds	Totals
Legislative, Judicial, Executive	$3,149	$2,875	$434	$6,458
State and Consumer Services	598	748	24	1,370
Business, Transportation & Housing	905	7,304	4,294	12,503
Natural Resources	2,108	2,427	849	5,384
Environmental Protection	77	1,101	294	1,472
Health and Human Services	26,346	11,157	174	37,677
Corrections and Rehabilitation	8,931	48	1	8,980
K-12 Education	36,079	81	684	36,844
Higher Education	11,490	36	1,095	12,621
Labor and Workforce Development	58	383	-	441
Non-Agency Departments	586	1,609	2	2,197
Tax Relief/Local Government	534	2,178	-	2,712
Statewide Expenditures	-4,309	904	-	-3,405
Total	**$86,552**	**$30,851**	**$7,851**	**$125,254**

---

[74] State Budget Highlights, California Department of Finance, October 2008.

101

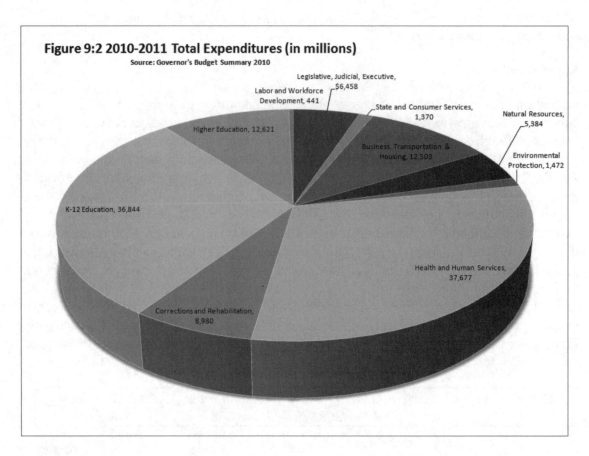

Figure 9:2 2010-2011 Total Expenditures (in millions)
Source: Governor's Budget Summary 2010

- Labor and Workforce Development, 441
- Legislative, Judicial, Executive, $6,458
- State and Consumer Services, 1,370
- Natural Resources, 5,384
- Higher Education, 12,621
- Business, Transportation & Housing, 12,503
- Environmental Protection, 1,472
- K-12 Education, 36,844
- Health and Human Services, 37,677
- Corrections and Rehabilitation, 8,980

Popular Input

Since this is Progressive California, the people have from time to time passed initiatives that affect the state's budget process. Most scholars agree that Proposition 13, the Jarvis Tax Revolt, was the most significant in terms of process; however, in terms of substance, Proposition 98 has been very powerful. Proposition 13 forced the state legislature to find supermajorities in order to pass a budget, and as discussed previously, has made agreement extremely difficult. Proposition 98 passed in 1988 guaranteed that the funding for kindergarten through community college education could not be decreased. The schools are to receive either the percentage of the budget they were receiving then or the actual number of dollars increased for inflation. The community colleges receive some of those dollars, typically about 10 percent. In difficult fiscal times, these limitations have caused problems for the state.

This year's budget problems present tremendous threats to California's economic well-being. Along with the rest of the country, California is feeling the devastating effects of the bank collapses, unemployment, and housing market crashes. According to Legislative Analyst Mac Taylor, of the nonpartisan Legislative Analyst's Office (LAO), state expenses are rising, Here is an excerpt of his assessment of the budget issues from January 2010 before the budget passed in October 2010. "The Governor proposes $19.9 billion of budget solutions in 2009-10 and 2010-11 to address the budget shortfall and create a $1 billion reserve. While it is reasonable to assume the state will secure some new federal funding and flexibility, the chances that the state will receive all of what the Governor seeks from Washington are almost non-existent. The Legislature should assume that federal relief will be billions of dollars less than the Governor wants— necessitating that it make more very difficult decisions affecting both state revenues and spending. Many of this year's budget solutions will require significant time for departments to implement. Therefore, the Legislature and the Governor need to agree to a framework to solve much of the budget problem by the end of March."[75]

CALIFORNIA'S INSTITUTIONS OF HIGHER EDUCATION

California's academic institutions of higher education are under constant threat of budget cuts and increases in student fees. The 2008–2009 budget reflected this situation. The governing boards for both the University of California (UC) and California State University (CSU) approved increases for student fees. Students and faculty raised opposition to the proposed hikes, but the boards voted to raise tuition for the sixth year since 2001. Undergraduate fees for UC have increased to $7,126 (7.4 percent) and to $3,048 (10 percent) for CSU. Graduate fees for both UC and CSU have also increased by 7.4 percent and 10 percent respectively. In the last six years, student fees have doubled. The fee increase is likely to hurt lower- and middle-income students the hardest, who are already working up to and above 40 hours a week.

According to the Governor's Budget Summary on Higher Education, while the budget does not provide additional enrollment growth funding, the segments plan to meet or exceed the budgeted levels of instruction delivery funded in 2007–2008. The University of California will continue to accept all qualified students despite being overenrolled by over 4,000 full time enrolled (FTE) students in 2007–2008. The CSU "appears to be sustaining over enrollments in 2008–2009 of 8,000 FTE students." While the budget summary analyzes the capacity, it does not analyze quality as students struggle to find classes and professors face severe increases in class size and course loads.

The Public Policy Institute finds that Californians are worried about the future of California's institutions of higher education. Their main concern is the cost of attending university in California, and they are looking to the state to help out. However, "most state residents would balk at paying higher taxes to prevent funding cuts for higher education."[76] While the survey notes that "California's public colleges are widely considered a bargain," the savings are offset by the enormous costs of living in California.

LOCAL GOVERNMENT

Local government has been tremendously impacted by popular initiatives. Thirty years ago, the best source of income for cities and schools was the property tax, a tax levied against the value of the property. In the inflationary 70s, however, this tax escalated at an alarming rate, particularly for those on fixed incomes. A taxpayer revolt in 1978 in the

---

[75] Mac Taylor Budget Overview, http://www.lao.ca.gov/laoapp/main.aspx?type=2&PubTypeID=2
[76] Holland, Gale 2008 "California budget crisis has residents worrying about state college costs," *Lost Angeles Times* November 14, 2008

form of the initiative Proposition 13 rolled back property taxes and severely limited their future growth. The void has been filled by an increased dependence on the state and more active pursuit of businesses that provide sales tax. Before Proposition 13, a typical school district received a limited amount of federal money, with the rest of its income divided about evenly between state and local property tax sources. Today, most of the money and, of course, contro, comes from the state. Cities fight over automobile dealerships and large retail stores that produce significant sales tax revenue.

Income

As a group, counties receive most of their money from other levels of government. Remember that they serve as local administrators for many state and federal programs. A typical county receives over 40 percent of its income from the state and over 20 percent from the federal government. Other sources are property taxes, service charges, and sales tax.

Cities have a different pattern of income. A typical city derives about 40 percent of its income from service charges, such as charges for trash, sewage, electricity, and water. State and federal revenues account for another 13 percent or so, followed by sales and use taxes, property taxes, utility taxes, and a myriad of smaller taxes.

Expenditures

According to the state controller, a typical county spends its money public assistance (welfare), public protection, health and sanitation, administration and elections, roads, and other smaller categories. A typical city spends its money on public safety, community development and health, public utilities, transportation, parks, recreation and libraries, and general government.

FINANCING LOCAL GOVERNMENT: THE CASE OF THE OAKLAND RAIDERS

Across the nation, local governments seeking both revenue and civic pride have spent millions of dollars to lure professional sports teams. Some studies show a tremendous infusion of capital into the local economy from these ventures, although some of the assumptions may be a bit questionable. Before making the commitment, however, cities should consider the case study of Oakland and its Raiders.

The Oakland Raiders were a very successful professional football team in the 1970s and 80s. Looking for greener pastures, however, owner Al Davis moved the team to Los Angeles. Oakland's pride was stung, and the city continued to look for ways to bring the National League team back. Finally, in 1997, after a 14-year stay in Los Angeles, the team returned triumphantly to the Bay Area. The move, however, has turned out to be a disaster and should stand as a warning to other municipalities.

It is an important factor that the Raiders of the 1990s were not a particularly good football team. Fans will pay exorbitantly to see a successful team but stay away from a losing one. Furthermore, many low-income people populate the Oakland-Alameda County area. There is also competition from the San Francisco 49ers across the bay.

Nevertheless, the city made an extraordinary effort to retrieve the Raiders. It issued $200 million in bonds to finance a major expansion of the Oakland-Alameda County Coliseum and basically guaranteed Mr. Davis that the team would not lose money. To quiet opposition, city officials promised that no money would come from the general fund. Instead, season ticket holders were required to purchase personal seat licenses (PSLs) and pay annual maintenance fees just for the privilege of being able to buy game tickets. The PSLs ranged in price from $250 to $4,000, plus another $50 to $75 in annual fees. These monies were to be used to repay the principal and interest on the bonds.

To the surprise of no one outside Oakland, the campaign to sell the PSLs failed to meet the city's needs. Many of the seats were not good, the team was not good, and the licenses were only effective for 10 years. Fortunately, the Raiders began to improve and even earned a Super Bowl bid in 2003. For now, the seats are full of happy and boisterous fans. Whether the gamble of public monies will pay off in the long run remains to be seen.

SOMETHING TO THINK ABOUT

1. How has the initiative process impacted California's spending on programs and other policies?

2. What challenges to California's educational system (K–12) must the state address? How does its multicultural and ethnic diversity impact its educational policy?

3. What are the implications of California's higher education policy on future college students in the state?

4. What problems are presented by the state's tax structure?

5. How has California's political culture impacted spending in the state?

6. What social service issues must California address as it enters the twenty-first century?

7. What are the major sources of revenue for the state of California?

MULTIPLE-CHOICE QUESTIONS

1) Public policies do all of the following EXCEPT
   a) reconcile conflicting claims on scarce resources.
   b) establish incentives for cooperation and collective action that would be irrational without government influence.
   c) remain silent on morally unacceptable behavior.
   d) protect the activity of a group or individual, promoting activities that are essential to government.
   e) provide direct benefits to citizens.

2) In terms of economic policy, California's process of allocation is complicated by
   a) its requirement that the legislature must present every budget item to the voters for approval.
   b) the grants California receives from the federal government in order to implement programs and policies the United States Congress has passed.
   c) the money that the counties pay back to the state for funding of local programs.
   d) the requirement that the state legislature pass budget bills unanimously.
   e) All of the above

3) Which of the following statements about the budget bill is true?
   a) It is prepared by the State Controller's Office.
   b) The governor refines a draft of the bill and submits it to the legislature by July 1.
   c) It must balance revenues and spending, a result of a constitutional amendment requiring a balanced budget.
   d) It must be passed unanimously by the state legislature.
   e) The governor must either veto the entire bill or sign it; this explains why California frequently misses the deadline for the bill, as it did in 2008–2009, when the bill passed on September 23, 2008.

4) The state's budget income
   a) comes mostly from taxes on large corporations and banks.
   b) is collected by the Board of Equalization.
   c) comes mostly from retail sales taxes.
   d) comes mostly from individual personal income taxes.
   e) is collected by the Internal Revenue Service.

5) In terms of expenditures, the state spends the majority of its funds on
   a) K–12 education.
   b) health and human services.
   c) higher education.
   d) prisons and law enforcement.
   e) the various branches of government.

6) One of the greatest influences on the budget is Proposition 98. Passed in 1988, it
    a) guaranteed that the funding for kindergarten through community college education could not be decreased.
    b) required that revenues and expenditures must be balanced.
    c) guaranteed funding for higher education will stay constant at 10 percent.
    d) has meant reducing local property taxes (as Governor Wilson did during his administration).
    e) All of the above

7) With regard to education in the state of California,
    a) UC and CSU students have experienced a fee hike of nearly 10 percent in six years.
    b) K–12 has experienced significant cuts over the last six years.
    c) UC and CSU student fees will increase by 7 percent and 10 percent respectively for the academic year 2008–2009.
    d) A and C only
    e) A, B, and C

8) Passed in 1978, Proposition 13
    a) rolled back property taxes and severely limited their future growth.
    b) responded to the inflation of the 1970s that escalated taxes.
    c) changed the source of school district funding from largely state and local tax sources to state and federal resources.
    d) A and B only
    e) A, B, and C

9) Counties are funded primarily through
    a) federal and state revenue.
    b) local property taxes.
    c) sales taxes.
    d) income tax.
    e) service charges and for-use fees.

10) California's budget process is primarily influenced by
    a) the director of the Department of Finance.
    b) the global economy.
    c) initiatives, which have changed the procedures for allocating funds and passing the budget.
    d) the governor's party affiliation.
    e) federal grants to California to fulfill federal law.

INTERNET SOURCES
Department of Finance: **http://www.dof.ca.gov**
California Budget Project: **http://www.cbp.org**
Budget Documents: **http://www.dof.ca.gov/Budget/BudgetDocuments.asp**
The Budget Process: **http://www.dof.ca.gov/fisa/bag/process.htm**

ANSWER KEY FOR MULTIPLE-CHOICE QUESTIONS

Chapter 1
1. e
2. b
3. a
4. c
5. e
6. d
7. a
8. c
9. e
10. a

Chapter 2
1. a
2. d
3. e
4. b
5. a
6. b
7. c
8. e
9. e
10. c

Chapter 3
1. e
2. d
3. e
4. b
5. b
6. a
7. a
8. d
9. b
10. c

Chapter 4
1. e
2. d
3. a
4. c
5. e
6. b
7. d
8. d
9. d
10. b

Chapter 5
1. b
2. c
3. e
4. e
5. d
6. c
7. c
8. e
9. b
10. a

Chapter 6
1. b
2. c
3. c
4. e
5. a
6. d
7. e
8. e
9. b
10. a

0Chapter 7
1. d
2. b
3. e
4. c
5. e
6. a
7. e
8. d
9. b
10. e

Chapter 8
1. a
2. c
3. e
4. b
5. c
6. e
7. c
8. a
9. e
10. c

Chapter 9
1. c
2. b
3. c
4. d
5. a
6. a
7. c
8. e
9. a
10. c